DOING PSYCHOTHERAPY
EFFECTIVELY

DOING PSYCHOTHERAPY EFFECTIVELY

Mona Sue Weissmark
&
Daniel A. Giacomo

THE UNIVERSITY
OF
CHICAGO PRESS
Chicago & London

MONA SUE WEISSMARK is associate professor of psychology at Roosevelt University. DANIEL A. GIACOMO is medical director of outpatient psychiatry and assistant professor of psychiatry at the University of Chicago.

THE UNIVERSITY OF CHICAGO PRESS, CHICAGO 60637
THE UNIVERSITY OF CHICAGO PRESS, LTD., LONDON
© 1998 by The University of Chicago
All rights reserved. Published 1998
Printed in the United States of America

07 06 05 04 03 02 01 00 99 98   1 2 3 4 5

ISBN: 0-226-89167-4

Library of Congress Catologing-in-Publication Data

Weissmark, Mona Sue.
    Doing psychotherapy effectively / Mona Sue Weissmark and Daniel A.
Giacomo.
        p. cm.
    Includes bibliographical references and index.
    ISBN 0-226-89167-4 (alk. paper)
    1. Psychotherapy—Philosophy.   2. Psychotherapy—Evaluation.
3. Psychotherapist and patient.   4. Similarity judgment.
I. Giacomo, Daniel A.   II. Title.
RC437.5.W46   1998
616.89'14—dc21   97-25027
                                                        CIP

Portions of chapter 5 appeared in Mona Sue Weissmark and Daniel A. Giacomo, "Measuring Therapeutic Interactions: Research and Clinical Applications," Psychiatry, Interpersonal and Biological Processes 58, no. 2 (1995): 173–87. Reprinted by permission of Guilford Press.

In memory of my father,
ADOLF WEISSMARK,
20 March 1919–21 April 1994
Concentration Camp Survivor #184879
The most loving person I have ever known.
And for my mother,
STEFA WEISSMARK,
Concentration Camp Survivor #47021

To my parents,
ALFREDO AND LEONILDA,
sine qua nons.

To our teacher,
ARON KATSENELINBOIGEN,
to whose work this is only a footnote.

And for our daughter,
BRITTANY WEISSMARK GIACOMO

Contents

Acknowledgments

I am grateful to Aron Katsenelinboigen. My debt to Aron goes far back to when I was a doctoral student at the University of Pennsylvania. His courses on social systems inspired me to think about the problem of decision making in situations of uncertainty, uniqueness, and value conflict. From Aron I learned to think about my thinking.

My gratitude to Brendan Maher also is far-ranging. When I was a postdoctoral fellow and then a lecturer at Harvard, Brendan was a cherished source of intellectual support and challenge. He engaged me in dialogue on my research and offered illuminating perspectives and examples from his own—as well as invaluable methodological consulting. From Brendan I learned how to test my thinking.

I thank Jill Hooley, Robert Rosenthal, Ellen Langer, Jerome Kagan, and Myron Belfer, also at Harvard. They were helpful in vital ways, including reading and commenting on parts of early drafts, giving examples from their experience, discussing statistical and theoretical ideas with me, and helping me get the project funded. Although I list them together, each person's contribution is individually appreciated.

I also thank Hans H. Strupp for making available transcripts of therapy sessions and outcome from the Vanderbilt Psychotherapy Project.

And I thank David Brent, senior editor at the University of Chicago Press, who believed in the book from its inception.

Finally, I am grateful to Jonathan Smith, director of the School of Psychology at Roosevelt University, the students who have listened and contributed to my developing ideas, and my colleagues for providing me with a supportive academic home.

To my husband and coauthor, Daniel A. Giacomo, thank you for everything.

Mona Sue Weissmark

The thought and work leading to this book spread over many years, with the help and support of many people. I owe a special debt to Fidel

Lebensohn, who inspired me to pursue a career in psychiatry. Also, I owe much to Aron Katsenelinboigen. When I was a psychiatric resident at the University of Pennsylvania he had a strong influence on the direction of my research. John Brendler, Michael Silver, and Charles Fishman, also at the University of Pennsylvania, encouraged me to pursue my research interests. And Salvador Minuchin and Braulio Montalvo were very helpful in showing me how competent therapists work.

Many people at Harvard were also helpful. My special gratitude to Myron Belfer, who helped me secure a grant from the Harvard University Milton Fund and who willingly read the manuscript. Also, Michael Dodd and Harry Senger read early drafts of some of the chapters and provided helpful suggestions.

Finally, at the University of Chicago, a special word of thanks goes to Bennett Leventhal for reading the final version of the manuscript and to the students and residents who have listened to and challenged my developing ideas. Also, special thanks to David Brent, senior editor at the University of Chicago Press, for his commitment to seeing this book published.

Finally, thanks to my wife and coauthor, Mona Sue Weissmark, for her endless love.

Daniel A. Giacomo

Introduction

Theory versus Practice

Fourteen years ago, as a University of Pennsylvania doctoral student and a psychiatry resident, we undertook for a project some research on how therapists make decisions during therapy sessions. We discovered that the way in which decisions were being made in clinical settings bore little relation to the rational, theoretical accounts we had found in our psychotherapy books.

There is a difference between *theorizing* about therapy and *doing* therapy. Everyone who has tried to learn from a book how to play tennis, or write a story, or conduct therapy understands that difference. There is always a gap between theories and the reality to which they refer.

Theories for doing therapy can be useful, but they fail to determine the practice of therapy, for there are many factors to consider in practice that are left out of theoretical accounts. Theories can serve as a guide for action only if they can be integrated into the practical knowledge of doing therapy.

In the real world, the way therapists practice depends on the clinical situation. Most therapists do not cleave rigidly to the dictates of a theory, but rather act according to intuition, personal preference, the needs of their patient, and the problem at hand. Improvisation typifies any therapeutic encounter.

To the extent that the spontaneity of therapists' actions is considered crucial, it is evident that theory-based knowledge cannot account for clinical competence. Theories are static and context-free; therapists' actions are dynamic and context-dependent. This gap between theory and practice is reflected in the discussions between practitioners and researchers.

Practitioners argue that the perspectives of researchers are overly simplified and fail to address the needs of the day-to-day, in-session struggles of therapists and patients. They say they derive little guidance from the research literature. Practitioners claim that doing therapy involves dealing with situations of uncertainty and with the here and now.

Researchers counter that practitioners naively are trusting their own intuitions. They argue that practitioners are poorly equipped and uninformed in their efforts to help patients and suggest that scientific information is the avenue to correcting their misguided efforts. Researchers claim that the process of therapy must be measurable to be an effective method of treatment.

Practitioners reply that researchers are missing the point. The problem, they say, is not whether practitioners should rely on hard measurable facts or soft intuitions. The real problem, they argue, is failing to appreciate the *knowledge that arises from practice.* If one wishes to study the psychology of mathematics one studies the work of trained and gifted mathematicians, with emphasis on the decision making they use to give form to their mathematical intuitions. Likewise, practitioners argue, one does well to study the work of expert practitioners if one is to understand what competent practitioners actually do.

Researchers admit that more work needs to be done on what it is practitioners actually do. Part of the problem, researchers say, is that whereas most professionals recognize good practitioners when they see them, research has been slow to define and operationalize excellence in a systematic way. The difficulty, they say, is that knowledge that arises from practice has, to date, remained unspecifiable. "Clinicians' judgments are a function of a process we cannot trace," say researchers.

In the end, practitioners and researchers agree that an approach to psychotherapy research that parallels the decision-making process of expert practitioners would provide useful knowledge. Indeed, both practitioners and researchers recognize the value of clinical observations and judgments. Since the clinical decision is the most critical for doing therapy effectively, practitioners and researchers agree that it is at the very heart of a science of psychotherapy.

Despite the realization that doing psychotherapy involves knowledge that arises from practice, little progress has been made in specifying what competent therapists actually do. The way the clinician arrives at a decision still remains quasi-rational, nonrepeatable, and unexplainable. Some of it is so unexplainable that it has been called "intuition" or "good judgment." When people use terms such as "intuition" and "good judgment," it is as though they are saying, "The clinical method is indescribable." It is hardly surprising, therefore, that critics are increasingly questioning the legitimacy of psychotherapy and its efficacy as a curative tool. Psychotherapy often is viewed as quackery rather than as a scientifically tested treatment form.

Does Psychotherapy Work?

It is ironic that these concerns have been raised just as psychotherapy researchers have made much progress in demonstrating that psychotherapy works. Researchers have repeatedly shown that patients with diverse problems who receive a broad range of therapies improve more than they would with no treatment, with placebo treatment, or through spontaneous recovery. The benefits of therapy also compare favorably with those yielded by antidepressant drugs. In fact, the impact of psychotherapy often equals or exceeds the effects of other educational or medical efforts.

Knowing that psychotherapy works, however, does not explain how therapeutic interventions accomplish their effects. At first, researchers thought that some therapies worked better than others. They thought that the unique techniques of a particular therapy were the crucial components responsible for therapeutic effects, but researchers have been unsuccessful in their efforts to prove some therapeutic interventions work better than others. With few exceptions, researchers have failed, in study after study, to demonstrate the superiority of any major therapeutic school.

How Does Psychotherapy Work?

So scientists have been left to grapple with the question "If no one technique can claim superiority, what makes therapy successful?"

THE THERAPEUTIC ALLIANCE

The answer, researchers are discovering, seems to lie in the relationship between therapist and patient. Over the past two decades, the data show that success in therapy has much to do with the chemistry between therapist and patient and with the strength of the *working alliance* (also called *helping alliance* or *therapeutic alliance*). The working alliance generally is defined as the ability of therapist and client to work together in a collaborative relationship based on mutual trust, liking, and commitment to the work of therapy. Studies suggest that in most cases, the signs of a promising relationship are present within the first few sessions.

WHAT ALLIANCE STUDIES LEAVE OUT

Although studies on the alliance are important for highlighting the association between relationship factors and treatment outcome, none of them can account for what takes place when therapy works well. The studies do not provide precise descriptions of participant actions intrinsic to relationship factors. They say little about the doing of specific things in therapy that seem to make a difference. One cannot use the findings as a basis for drawing conclusions about which specific patient and therapist actions will maximize a promising therapeutic relationship. Thus, despite extensive research, surprisingly little progress has been made in understanding or empirically demonstrating how the therapeutic relationship contributes to the success or failure of psychotherapy.

Many reviews have suggested this lack of progress is due to (a) inadequate conceptualizations of the therapeutic relationship and (b) methods of evaluating therapists' and patients' behaviors that are too global, imprecise, or clinically irrelevant. For instance, as mentioned before, researchers think the success of therapy depends on the therapist and patient's establishing a therapeutic alliance. Several global methods for rating this relationship factor have been developed.

In general, global methods use frequency counts for rating the presence or absence of unidimensional and static variables. They are aimed at measuring the post hoc level of the overall alliance. Typically, judges read excerpts of therapy transcripts and rate the number of times particular positive or negative items occur. For example, judges are asked to rate the overall relationship climate with items such as "warmth" or "judgmentalness."

Although global methods have provided useful descriptive accounts that serve in a general sense to distinguish good from poor relationships, they do not specify what the therapist *does* to establish the quality of the relationship. Global methods thus may encourage the view that the relationship is just a generic factor unrelated to specific therapeutic actions.

Clinical inferences drawn from studies using such methods are similar to the methods from which they derive. They are global, static, and unidimensional. For instance, clinicians are advised to be less "strategic," "manipulative," and "instrumental" and more "collaborative," "flexible," "empathic," and "validating."

These qualities are thought to refine a therapist's relationships skills and improve the ability to facilitate a patient's progress in therapy. They say nothing, however, about what a therapist should *do* during the moment-to-moment changes in the patient-therapist relationship. It is easy to suggest that a competent therapist should establish a therapeutic alliance or be more empathetic and validating with a patient, but it is much more difficult to define precisely which therapist actions will best achieve such a goal.

DEFINING CRITICAL THERAPISTS' BEHAVIORS

Consequently, a crucial task of psychotherapy research is the development of a method that specifies what the therapist actually does to establish a therapeutic relationship. A method that can describe in-therapy performance is an important goal because it will enable reliable description of the therapeutic relationship at a level of clinical relevance. There is a growing consensus in the field that what is needed is a method that (a) identifies specific therapist actions that impact outcome, (b) uses an operational research language that is not theoretically specific (that uses everyday English) to permit comparisons across therapies, and (c) quantifies patterns of interactions between therapist and patient.

Developing a Method That Defines What Therapists Do

To this end, ten years ago, as a Harvard University postdoctoral fellow (and lecturer) and a Harvard Medical School psychiatrist, we undertook research on what therapists actually *do* to impact patients' changes. During videotaped studies of expert psychotherapists of different schools, we discovered that by attending to therapists' behaviors at the level of practice (as opposed to post hoc theoretical explanations) similar actions could be observed. That is to say, we discovered that despite differences in technique and theory, at the level of practice, therapists used the same operation to induce patients' changes.

Our next task was to develop a measure that operationalizes the therapists' operations and the patients' changes. Since our overall aim was to develop a measure that predicted treatment outcome and was clinically relevant, we needed to develop variables to measure aspects of therapists' behaviors that facilitate or impede progress in therapy. Likewise, we needed to develop variables to measure aspects of patients' behaviors that shift or remain stable during treatment. Also, if the measure was going to be useful for comparing different therapists, the variables needed to cut across theoretical orientations.

With the help of Brendan Maher, who was then chairman of Harvard's department of psychology, we developed the Harvard Psychotherapy Coding Method (HPCM). The HPCM operationalizes, in everyday English, the manner in which people organize their relational experiences during therapy. In later work we used the HPCM to conduct a process-outcome study. The study demonstrated that there is a direct relationship between what therapists do or fail to do during treatment and clinical outcome. Effective psychotherapy is not something mysterious or magical in which "anything goes." On the contrary, our study showed that the process of a successful psychotherapy follows a patterned set of operations.

What's *Doing Psychotherapy Effectively* About?

The purpose of this book is to describe the therapists' operations and the impact they have on patients' changes. *Unlike other psychotherapy books, it focuses on what actually takes place when therapy works well,* showing readers how to use their intuitive knowledge more rigorously and effectively. *Doing Psychotherapy Effectively* offers readers a variety of case examples illustrating the application of the HPCM to different schools of therapy. Above all an accessible, practical book, *Doing Psychotherapy Effectively* presents readers with a tool for measuring their effectiveness. As readers will note, our interest in this book, as it has been in our training and teaching sessions, is not to promote yet another school but to offer a basis on which each therapist can build and develop further improvements and refinements.

The book also focuses on patients' changes, showing readers what takes place when a human being succeeds in overcoming feelings of detachment, ineffectiveness, and rigidity and becomes more involved, effective, and adaptable. We show that it has much to do with the interaction between therapist and patient. There is a specific kind of interaction—one that increases patients' active participation—that is the essence of effective psychotherapy.

Doing Psychotherapy Effectively enables readers to see this process at work, and it suggests how we might better foster it in the training of future therapists. As Freud has suggested, "Is it not a justifiable endeavor on the part of a physician to seek to control the mental factor, to use it with a purpose, and to direct and strengthen it? This and nothing else is what scientific psychotherapy proposes."

Readers will finish this book with valuable tools to assist in doing psychotherapy effectively. Most important, the tools and operations in this book can be adapted to every kind of therapy. *Doing Psychotherapy Effectively* transcends the differences among psychotherapies, focusing on how therapists work rather than on theory.

Chapter 1 provides a brief history of psychotherapy research. We explore the reasons why traditional psychotherapy research has failed to answer the critical question "What makes therapy successful?" The major point we make is that there is a gap between research-based descriptions of psychotherapy and the practice of psychotherapy. The gap exists because the knowledge presented in research-based descriptions of psychotherapy is unlike the kind of knowledge practitioners use in practice.

Chapter 2 examines the differences between these two types of knowledge. We call the first *knowing-in-theory* and the second *knowing-in-practice*. We note that both researchers and practitioners agree that doing therapy involves more than applying theory-based knowledge. Both camps recognize that in clinical practice competent practitioners rely on another source of knowledge—their practical knowledge (their knowing-in-practice).

Despite this recognition, little progress has been made in bridging the gap between research and practice. We argue that a possible explanation for this lack of progress is that the thinking processes behind therapists' clinical knowledge remain unexplainable. Some of this knowledge is so vague it is called "intuition" or "good judgment."

In order to advance our understanding of the kind of knowing in which competent therapists engage, we describe two types of thinking. We call the first *logical thinking* and the second *analogical thinking*. In our discussion, we note that a key feature of analogical thinking is similarity. One thing reminds us of another. We see this as that.

In clinical practice the perception of similarity is essential. Using analogical reasoning the psychotherapist perceives a thematic similarity between the patient's story about the past and what is going on currently in the patient's life. Or the psychotherapist perceives that one case (or situation) is like another case he or she already encountered. Or the psychotherapist perceives what is common to classes of cases. In all these instances, we argue, the psychotherapist is perceiving a relation of likeness.

The ability to perceive different kinds of similarities is a basic tool of the therapist. We point out, however, that what the field of psychotherapy still lacks is a systematic method of determining similarity. What accounts for the therapist's perception of similarity? What do therapists "see" when they perceive similarities between patients' stories or situations that on the surface may be very different?

To address these questions, chapter 3 deals with how people in general and therapists in particular perceive similarities. We distinguish between two types of similarity perceptions: attributional similarity and relational similarity. This distinction focuses on the fact that one can perceive two stories, or two situations, as similar in terms of simple surface attributes. They could also be viewed as similar along deep relational attributes.

We then focus our discussion on relational attributes. We illustrate how people use relations to describe behavior and to assess what a behavior means. We show that similar relations can be applied to different behaviors and situations. For example, a person may assess as "intrusion" her child's entering her room, her husband's reading her mail, or her supervisor's asking her about her intimate life.

After our discussion of how similarities in general are perceived, a discussion needed before one can understand how it applies to the therapeutic situation, we examine how therapists perceive relational similarities. We argue that therapists perceive similar relational assessments in the stories patients tell. Whether it is termed a "thematic similarity," a "maladaptive assumption," a "person-schema," or a "core conflict," we argue, the therapist notices a relational affinity between the different stories the patient tells.

For instance, a patient arrives late to a psychotherapy session, then tells a story about her difficulties in completing a work assignment on time. The therapist is reminded of stories the patient has told in other sessions showing how her father criticized her and how she devised strategies for defeating him (Edelson, 1994). The psychotherapist notices a relational affinity between these stories about the past, what is going on currently in her work life, and the situation the patient seems to be enacting in the psychotherapy session. The particular characters, behaviors, and facts involved are different, yet the therapist identifies a similar relational structure between the stories. Feeling criticized and feeling unable to complete a work assignment are different kinds of things—and the behaviors performed are different kinds of actions. But both stories carry with them implicitly the relation "dominance" that the therapist perceives as similar.

In chapter 4, we further explore how individuals assess relational similarities. We begin by showing that relational assessments are multidimensional evaluations. Three crucial dimensions on which relations are assessed are the external-internal, the reactive-selective, and the unconditional-conditional. The evaluation of these dimensions bears on the meaning one gives to one's relational assessments. For example, it makes a great deal of difference whether one feels powerless to change a relationship (reactive) or whether one believes one can effect changes through one's own efforts (selective).

Next, we describe how a person's relational assessments evolve over time. We illustrate what assessing relations means in everyday interactions with other people. We then distinguish between two kinds of assessment styles: the passive observant profile and the active participatory profile. We conclude by showing that sometimes a person gets stuck in a fixed assessment style.

In chapter 5, we examine how therapy can help people shift their assessments from a passive observant profile to an active participatory profile. We describe how the Harvard Psychotherapy Coding Method can be used to quantify the dynamics of the therapeutic process. We present data showing that the therapeutic process of a successful therapy can be distinguished from the process of an unsuccessful therapy. Patients of a successful therapy shift their relational assessments (from early to late in therapy) so that they are significantly more internal, selective, and conditional, whereas patients of an unsuccessful therapy do not significantly change their assessments.

In presenting these data, we offer an operational definition of psychotherapy precise enough to specify therapists' behaviors and flexible enough to describe the different ways that psychotherapy actually is practiced. This feature, we suggest, will help narrow the gap between research and practice.

Chapter 6 shows the application of the method to different schools of therapy. It illustrates the method by offering extensive excerpts of dialogue from each of three cases: a cognitive case, a supportive-expressive case, and an interpersonal case. The concluding section is devoted to discussing directions for using the method in practice, in training, and in future research.

We hope that readers will enjoy the glimpses into our research, question its conclusions thoughtfully, and test the implications in their own lives. Because there is less of a spirit of competition between different schools of therapy, less of a spirit of "either your theory or mine" among those wanting to advance the practice of psychotherapy, we think the time is right for going beyond sectarianism and ideology by focusing on therapists' actions, on what different techniques and theories may have in common at the level of practice. To quote Freud (1904, p. 252), "There are many ways and means of practicing psychotherapy. All that lead to recovery are good."

We hope that the work reported here will provide greater insight into what makes therapy effective and will serve as a useful point of departure for future work, both empirical and theoretical.

1

A Brief History of Psychotherapy Research

"I knew I had problems," says a thirty-six-year-old woman of her one-year experience in psychotherapy. "I knew that something was crippling me, keeping me from moving forward, and from having satisfying relationships. The therapist was incredibly perceptive. He could sum things up in one sentence, and tell me where they were connected. He had this way of asking me questions that made me look at things differently. I still have some of the same problems, but I see them differently now. Life is more manageable now, and I feel I have more choices."

The Role of the Case Study

Fifty years ago, any evidence that psychotherapy worked rested largely on such personal testimonials. People who were in therapy said it helped and therapists saw clients improve. Therapists documented the cases, described their procedures, and discussed them with colleagues. Hypotheses attributing success or failure to various assumed causes came from these cases. Gradually these hypotheses grew into theories of psychotherapy.

As Hersen and Barlow (1976, p. 9) point out, the theories multiplied, and procedures based on observations of cases and inferences from these theories grew in number. Those theories that were conveyed clearly or that presented new and exciting views tended to attract followers, and schools of psychotherapy were formed. At the heart of this process is the uncontrolled case study method of investigation. This was the main methodology of clinical investigation through the first half of the twentieth century.

The case study played a key role in clinical psychology. Indeed, understanding of the individual is thought to be a distinguishing trait of clinical psychology. The case study of the individual client has contributed to knowledge in several areas of clinical work. Modern psychiatric diagnosis began with the careful analysis and collection of individual cases (Kraepelin, 1883). Information about rare disorders such as multiple personality has come essentially from careful in-depth descriptions of individual cases. The history of many psychotherapy techniques and conceptual models can be traced to the influence of one or a few cases. Examples include the cases of Dora, the Rat Man, Little Hans, the Wolf-Man, Schreber, Anna O., Little Albert, and Peter (Kazdin, 1986).

Perhaps the greatest impact of the case study has been in the area of clinical training. In general, an "art" that cannot be specified in detail cannot be transmitted by prescription, since no prescription for it exists. It can be passed on from supervisor to student only by case examples. Advocates of case teaching claim that carefully guided analysis of particular clinical cases drawn from real treatment contexts helps a student develop the clinical skills essential to becoming an effective therapist. The large amount of time spent by students of clinical psychology, chemistry, biology, and medicine in their practical courses shows how greatly these sciences rely on the transmission of skills from teacher to student.

Although advocates of case teaching admit that they cannot define these skills, they believe that the case method stands on its own merits. They claim that it is a useful method for teaching students to apply theory and techniques to a particular case. By watching or discussing cases with an experienced therapist-supervisor, students can pick up the rules for doing psychotherapy, including those that are not explicitly known to the supervisor. Students follow their supervisors because they trust their manner of doing things even when they cannot analyze and account for its effectiveness. Although the case study has been recognized by many as a useful method for teaching clinical skills, as the science of psychology grew, investigators claimed that the case study was useless for studying the effectiveness of a treatment.

Does Psychotherapy Work? The Role of the Controlled Study

By the 1950s, with the arrival of applied research, investigators began to reject reports from uncontrolled case studies, claiming such reports could not be used to evaluate the effects of treatment. Because the case history was typically a condensed account summarizing many hours of therapy, it relied on anecdotal information, such as clinical impressions, judgments, and inferences, that tended to be influenced by the clinicians' speculations and appeals to theory.

Although a therapist may have attributed client improvement to the theoretical constructs underlying the therapy that was provided, researchers claimed that it was possible that other factors not recognized by the therapist may have been the actual cause of client change. In the case study approach there is no way of checking the reliability of observations or the justification for particular inferences. Because the case study did not control for other factors, it did not provide much support for claims of the effectiveness of a particular treatment.

LIMITATIONS OF THE CASE STUDY

Studies without comparison groups, such as the uncontrolled case study, were considered among the weakest research designs. In order to evaluate the effectiveness of any treatment, it is essential to compare the outcome of patients who receive the treatment to that of other patients who do not receive the treatment. If one does not compare treated patients to untreated patients but just relies on the rhetorical impact of a reported treatment recovery rate, imagine the impact of reports of 90 percent success rates. Such high success rates might be obtained when treating patients suffering from the common cold (or other time-limited conditions) with some new dietary intervention (Wierzbicki, 1993). Should you conclude that diet improves a cold? You cannot know for sure. You have no way of knowing whether similar changes would have occurred had the participants not received the treatment. But if you were in the business of advertising for the diet company you might be motivated to say that curing colds with the new diet was a very successful form of treatment.

One wonders if the early development of clinical techniques would have been different if practitioners had been less motivated to form "schools" of therapy. Since all therapy procedures achieved some success, practitioners within the various schools focused on positive results, explained away the failures, and decided that the general results proved that their techniques were responsible for the successes.

Due to the strong and overriding belief in the theories central to each school, the successes were credited to theoretical constructs underlying the techniques. This prevented a precise analysis of elements in the therapeutic intervention that may have been responsible for changes in a given case. This also had the effect of supporting the application of a global, ill-defined treatment (from whatever theoretical orientation) to global definitions of behavior disorders, such as "neurosis." This, in turn, led to statements such as "Psychoanalytic therapy works with neurotics" or "Behavior therapy works with schizophrenics." The result was a collection of successful individual case studies, with clinicians from different schools claiming that their techniques were vital to success (Hersen and Barlow, 1976).

ATTITUDES TOWARD CONTROLLED STUDIES

The leap from uncontrolled case study to scientific investigation was not due to lack of awareness of basic scientific principles in early clinicians. Freud, for instance, worked in a physiology laboratory and did some high-quality research in microscopic neuroanatomy. Years later, after he founded psychoanalysis, however, Freud (1917/1963) rejected empirical research methods, stating that "statistics are worthless if the items assembled in them are too heterogeneous; and the cases of neurotic illness which we had taken into treatment were in fact incomparable in a great variety of respects" (p. 461). When Freud was presented with the results of ten years of cases conducted by the Berlin Psychiatric Institute, he replied that "statistics of that kind are in general uninstructive; the material worked upon is so heterogeneous that only very large numbers would show anything. It is wiser to examine one's individual experiences" (1933/1964, p. 152).

This attitude toward controlled studies of therapy continued to dominate the field of psychotherapy in the first half of the 1900s and was widely shared by proponents of different schools of therapy. For example, when Wertheimer asked for data addressing the effectiveness of humanistic therapy, a proponent of humanistic therapy had the following response: "In the first place, and perhaps most disturbing, these approaches are typically inimical to solid data: It is almost heretical, 'dehumanizing,' to raise a question about the effectiveness of these procedures . . ." (Wertheimer, 1978, p. 744).

Historically, therapists of different approaches resisted the notion that they must prove the value of what they do. Individual clinical judgment was the standard for deciding what clients needed and whether they were improving, and some therapists argued that any attempt to dissect what happens in therapy is misguided. The evaluation of change in human behavior, they said, is largely indescribable, an intricate interplay of qualities not easily specified, inevitably oversimplified by quantification.

When the *practice* of psychotherapy is defended more as an art than a science, the intent is to say that it is a highly developed set of skills that aim to produce effects. However, neither the skills nor the effects are sufficiently predictable or measurable to meet scientific standards. When people use terms such as *creative* and *intuitive* they usually mean to end discussion rather than to open up inquiry. It is as if the person says to his or her students and colleagues, "I know the practice of psychotherapy requires certain skills but any attempt to describe or measure them is impossible" (Giacomo and Weissmark, 1986; Polanyi, 1958).

A CHALLENGE TO THE FIELD

Gradually, however, skeptics appeared on the scene, challenging the believers to use rigorous procedures of verification. They argued that therapists had a responsibility to prove that therapy is effective. It should be a matter not of faith, conviction, or testimony but of reasonably well-established fact, they said. These scientists were quick to point out the drawbacks of the case study method in evaluating the effects of psychotherapy. Among them was British psychologist Hans Eysenck, who in a famous 1952 critique said that two-thirds of neurotic individuals got better—with or without therapy. Eysenck gave voice to what many skeptics had been thinking. He argued forcefully that there was no evidence that psychotherapy with neurotics was any more effective than no treatment at all.

Eysenck reviewed all the studies published to date that reported success rates of various types of psychotherapy. He limited his review to psychotherapy with "neurotics." Because the studies reviewed by Eysenck did *not* include control groups of untreated neurotics, he had to estimate the recovery rate of untreated neurotics. He did so by combining the results of two studies. The first was Landis's 1938 study, which reported on the percentage of neurotics in state hospitals who presumably did not receive therapy treatment; the second was Denker's 1946 study, which examined 500 cases of neurotics who saw general practitioners rather than mental health practitioners. Using these data, Eysenck reported that the expected recovery rate from neurosis without psychotherapy was 72 percent, compared with 66 percent with eclectic treatment and 44 percent with psychoanalysis.

Methodological criticisms of Eysenck's study were many and have often been quoted. However, the point we wish to emphasize here is that Eysenck's work issued a challenge to the field. Even if methodological criticisms completely invalidate Eysenck's argument, that still does not prove that patients treated with therapy had a more favorable outcome than untreated patients—any more than studies treating patients suffering from the common cold with a special diet prove that the new diet cures the common cold. If psychotherapy works, then researchers would have to show this empirically in controlled studies.

To say that Eysenck's argument is flawed does not substitute for providing empirical data from controlled experimental studies that show the effectiveness of psychotherapy. Eysenck himself noted that his data did not disprove the possibility of the effectiveness of therapy. He encouraged the field to gather more facts concerning the effectiveness of therapy and to conduct rigorous controlled studies that might support the claim that psychotherapy is effective. Eysenck's study reinforced the growing view that the effects of psychotherapy could not be evaluated from case reports and so sparked a new flurry of interest in evaluating psychotherapy through the scientific method.

REVIEWING THE CONTROLLED STUDIES

In response to Eysenck's charge, researchers started conducting controlled studies in which one form of therapy was compared either to no therapy or to another form of therapy. By the 1970s there were hundreds of studies—some showing that therapy was effective and others showing that therapy was ineffective. When different therapies were compared, the results were also inconsistent. Some studies showed no differences between different forms of therapy. Other studies suggested behavioral therapy was more effective than verbal therapy, and yet other studies suggested verbal therapy was more effective than behavioral therapy. When superiority was evident, the results were often attributed to the bias of researchers (Lambert, Shapiro, and Bergin, 1986).

Qualitative Reviews

How then could contradictory findings from different studies be resolved? Because the empirical literature became so extensive and contradictory, it was difficult for the professional to read and critically evaluate all the research. Difficulties in reconciling contradictory conclusions from similar studies cripple a fundamental component of the scientific process: the systematic accumulation of knowledge. As a result, literature reviews appeared. Such reviews examine a portion of the literature with the goals of summarizing the results, interpreting the findings, and making recommendations concerning the practice of therapy and the conduct of future studies. Unfortunately, literature reviews are scientifically unsound.

Reviewers differ in how they include and exclude, how they evaluate, and how they interpret the findings of studies. For example, Luborsky, Singer, and Luborsky (1975) reported that nineteen comparisons of behavior therapy and psychotherapy resulted in thirteen tie scores and six comparisons that favored behavior therapy. From this they concluded that there was no difference in effectiveness between the two types of therapy. Such a judgment is arbitrary because it is likely that an evaluator representing another point of view might come up with an entirely different conclusion. An alternative interpretation, equally supported by this comparison, was given by Kazdin and Wilson (1978). They pointed out that behavior therapy always equalled or surpassed psychotherapy. The authors then concluded that behavior therapy was more effective.

Qualitative surveys of the literature can often lead to conflicting conclusions when different investigators evaluate the same domains. Thus, literature reviews led to the same sort of problems as did personal testimonies about the effectiveness of therapy. Different reviewers reached different conclusions regarding the effectiveness of therapy in general and the relative efficacies of different forms of therapy, with followers of a specific school claiming favorable results for their form of therapy.

Quantitative Reviews

One response to these shortcomings was to use statistical procedures called meta-analytic techniques. Because these techniques make explicit the decisions made by the reviewer they are less subjective than literature reviews and are regarded as a more precise method of evaluating large bodies of research. Smith and Glass (1977) were the first researchers to use such a technique. They identified 475 experimental studies in which one form of therapy was compared either to no therapy or to another form of therapy. On average, they found, the psychotherapy client is better off than 80 percent of untreated control individuals, which seems to provide evidence of the efficacy of psychotherapy. Although this study is not without its critics, researchers have enough data to refute Eysenck's charge with conviction. There is now little doubt that therapy treatments are, in general, beneficial.

In fact, the impact of therapy often equals or surpasses the effects of other educational or medical efforts. Researchers have developed methods to assess the effects of psychotherapy change, broadly defined. They find the improvement in the health of therapy clients greater, for example, than the gains in reading of elementary-school students given nine months of reading instruction or than the effects of aspirin on heart attacks (Rosnow and Rosenthal, 1989). (See Rosenthal, 1983, for a clear presentation of computational formulas and for the "binomial effect size display" as a guide for communicating the practical consequences of treatment interventions.) The benefits of therapy also compare favorably with those yielded by antidepressant drugs. Still, some problems—addictions, for example—often recur, even with therapy. And some clients remain unmoved by therapy or even get worse. But, on the average, investigators have shown that clients who receive a broad range of therapies improve more than they would with no treatment, with placebo treatment, or through spontaneous recovery.

Beyond this global testimony to the effectiveness of therapy, investigators have been less successful in their efforts to discover whether some therapies work better than others. Smith and Glass (1977) concluded from their meta-analytic study that the evidence overwhelmingly supported the efficacy of therapy but that different types of therapy did *not* produce different benefits:

> We did not expect that the demonstrable benefits of quite different types of psychotherapy would be so little different. It is the most startling and intriguing finding we came across. All psychotherapy researchers should be prompted to ask how it can be so. If it is truly so that major differences in technique count for little in terms of benefits, then what is to be made of the volumes devoted to the careful drawing of distinctions among styles of psychotherapy? And what is to be made of the deep divisions and animosities among different psychotherapy schools? (p. 185)

Beyond Effectiveness: How Does Therapy Work?

To say that something worked (or failed) without saying what it was that made it work hinders an essential aspect of the scientific process—replicability. If a treatment is effective but the essential ingredients of the treatment cannot be determined and evaluated, then the treatment cannot be reproduced. Basing psychotherapy studies on ascribed or alleged treatments is equivalent to giving red and blue pills to patients in a drug study without knowing the active ingredients of the pills. Applying a global treatment such as psychotherapy to a heterogeneous group of clients classified under a vague diagnostic category such as neurosis leaves unanswered questions about the effectiveness of a specific treatment for a specific disorder. This realization led researchers to go beyond studying treatment efficacy to exploring how therapy works.

Questions about how psychotherapy works have been explored using different approaches. Generally, there have been two main ways of investigating the issue. We might call them the *unique specific approach* and the *common nonspecific approach*. We shall examine each of these in turn.

THE UNIQUE SPECIFIC APPROACH

This approach addresses the issue of how therapy works by carefully examining the unique differences among the therapies. According to this approach a major limitation of past studies (many of which showed no differences between treatments) is that past studies did not specify particular treatments and ensure that they were offered to patients in the prescribed manner. Therapists in comparative studies may have had different, unclear, or mistaken ideas of what each treatment consisted of and so didn't deliver the distinct treatment methods consistently (Stiles, Shapiro, and Elliott, 1986). "Thus, to ask whether psychotherapy is indeed therapeutic, and to attempt to answer that question by comparing behavioral or personality change in counseled and 'control' groups, is very much like a pharmacologist asking, 'Is chemotherapy therapeutic?' and then conducting his research by randomly giving unknown kinds and quantities of drugs to one group of patients with various complaints, and no drug to a similar 'control' group" (Truax and Carkhuff, 1967, p. 18).

According to the unique specific approach, past studies of therapy effectiveness incorrectly assumed that patients were undergoing a homogeneous set of treatment conditions and that therapists were delivering a homogeneous treatment. Such studies, according to the specific viewpoint, are almost meaningless because of variations in patients and types of therapeutic activities. According to this line of reasoning, the question "'Is psychotherapy effective?' is analogous to asking 'Is higher education effective?' without specifying what kind of higher education, practiced by what kind of teachers on which student" (Hyman and Breger, 1965, p. 319).

The unique specific approach asserts that a more useful way of addressing the question of how therapy works is to focus on particular types of therapy with certain types of patients. Whereas meta-analysis may have shown that therapy is better than no therapy, it has not established that different therapies engender equivalent benefits with respect to particular clinical problems or types of patients. Thus, according to the specific approach the focus of research should be on comparing standardized treatments for a particular clinical problem. The question addressed by the unique specific approach is, Which standardized treatment is better among various alternative modalities for a particular disorder?

Thus, if one wishes to test adequately the effects of specific treatment approaches, the approaches must be clearly defined and the therapists must carry out their respective treatment conditions in a competent and consistent fashion (Elkin, Pilkonis, Docherty, and Sotsky, 1988). If one wants to establish the generality of findings, one must use more adequate sampling procedures involving larger numbers of clients seen in many different settings by a variety of therapists—in other words, the "grand collaborative study" (Bergin and Strupp, 1972; Strupp and Luborsky, 1962).

This type of research strategy is exemplified by a recent project sponsored by the National Institute of Mental Health (NIMH). Two brief psychotherapies—interpersonal therapy and cognitive behavioral therapy—were compared (as well as two pharmacotherapies, imipramine plus clinical management and placebo plus clinical management) for the treatment of outpatient depression. Treatments were conducted at three research sites, where all sites used the same research strategy.

Specification, Identification, and Verification of the Unique Ingredients

Unlike the major comparative studies of the past, the NIMH Treatment of Depression Collaborative Research Program (TDCRP) focused particular attention on delineating and specifying the treatments. There was an increased emphasis on the "standardization" or "specification" of the technique variable. The concrete specification of treatment procedures was considered important not only to determine what had been done in the study at hand but also to enable replication of treatment in subsequent investigations and applications.

Therefore, a key feature of the study was standard training programs for the therapists in each of the treatment modalities. Experienced therapists were provided with training in the prescribed treatment techniques and were monitored for adherence to the techniques. Including standard training was thought to be a step toward correcting what was seen as a general failure in previous comparative studies—the lack of a clear definition of the therapeutic modalities studied (Elkin, Parloff, Hadley, and Autry, 1985). To ensure that the active ingredients in a treatment were actually being delivered, it was necessary to define carefully the treatment condition, including the nature of the therapist's interventions.

Most prominent among the methodological advances in this area was the development and use of manuals, which described and provided guidelines for the conduct of the particular forms of psychotherapy that were being compared—interpersonal and cognitive behavioral therapy (Elkin,

Pilkonis, Docherty, and Sotsky, 1988). A manual was defined broadly to include written materials designed to guide the therapists in the goals of treatment and in the procedures, techniques, topics, themes, therapeutic maneuvers, and other behaviors and activities that transpired over the course of treatment. The interpersonal therapy manual provided specific steps to deal with four interpersonal problem areas. Pathological grief, for example, required expressing feelings, clarifying problem reactions, mourning the loss, developing new relationships, and handling therapy termination (Klerman et al., 1984). In contrast, the cognitive behavioral manual offered a cognitive analysis of depression and prescribed techniques to change cognitive distortions and activities aimed at questioning basic assumptions. Homework assignments were integral to the therapy, and emphasis was placed on an analysis of automatic self-defeating thoughts occurring outside therapy (Beck et al., 1979).

The assumption was that the contents of the manual identified the unique ingredients of a particular therapy and that these unique ingredients were the crucial components responsible for therapeutic benefit. The specification, identification, and verification of the unique ingredients were considered essential for understanding the mechanisms through which different therapies might produce differential treatment outcomes. Researchers were hoping that "the identification and distillation of the most valued techniques of specific treatment approaches in a manual format, with its promise of greater specificity and differential treatment, may yet allow for a demonstration of differential psychotherapy outcome" (Lambert, Shapiro, and Bergin, 1986, p. 178).

Summary of Results

Contrary to expectations, the results showed *no* significant differences among the treatments for the less severely depressed patients (Elkin et al., 1989). Thus, although the unique specific approach was a major methodological advance over earlier global approaches (those that applied a global treatment to a heterogeneous group of clients classified under a vague diagnostic category), the conclusions reached were similar, namely, that the psychotherapies were an effective form of treatment but different types of psychotherapy did not produce significantly different benefits.

Researchers today are as puzzled as Smith and his colleagues were when they concluded that different therapies did not produce different benefits. The equal outcome phenomenon is considered by some to be the most consistent and striking finding in the psychotherapy research literature. That is not to say, of course, that all studies show this or that no differences in outcome exist, but rather that most results to date support the view that each approach is to some extent effective.

The NIMH study's findings, however, did not suffer from the same limitations as the existing research. Researchers could be more confident that a specific treatment was in fact being delivered to a specific diagnostic group. Therefore, they were assured that different techniques, as specified by the manuals, were being applied. Yet, the findings demonstrated that one could *not* conclude with equal confidence that the techniques were the sought-after active ingredients of the treatment. In terms of the pharmacological analogy, there was no demonstration that the specified techniques were the active ingredients or that nonmanualized aspects of the therapeutic interactions were inert. We might say, therefore, that researchers advanced in distinguishing "red from blue pills"; but it appeared evident that knowing the difference between red and blue pills did not account for the active ingredients of the pills.

Although researchers have determined the differential procedural ingredients of different interventions, they still have not identified which of the various ingredients are active. Thus, the question remains, "What is effectively therapeutic about psychotherapy?" (Orlinsky and Howard, 1986, p. 311). Or put another way, what therapeutic procedures or processes produce positive change in the client? Given that over the years there has been little evidence to support the view that greater specificity and differential treatment allow for a demonstration of differential psychotherapy outcomes, there was room for another approach regarding how psychotherapeutic interventions accomplish their effects.

THE COMMON NONSPECIFIC APPROACH

An alternative approach espoused by many authors is the common nonspecific approach. This approach addresses the issue of how therapy works by searching for common ingredients among the therapies. Whereas the unique specific approach emphasizes the specification of differences, the common nonspecific approach seeks to abstract similarities (at the level of theory or practice) across different therapies.

The suggestion that there are underlying similarities linking seemingly different psychotherapies was made as early as 1936 (Rosenzweig, 1936). Rosenzweig pointed to several factors that he believed might account for the effectiveness of different therapies. These included the therapist's ability to inspire hope and the importance of providing the patient with different ways of viewing the self and the world. During the next forty years occasional publications on the topic appeared. Since 1980, however, there has been an increase in interest in the common factors approach, with more books and papers published during these years than all previous years combined (for example, Beutler, 1983; Brady et al., 1980; Cornsweet, 1983; Garfield, 1980; Goldfried, 1980; Grencavage and Norcross, 1990; Haaga, 1986; Jones, Cumming, and Horowitz, 1988; Karasu, 1986; Lambert, 1986; Orlinsky and Howard, 1987; Prochaska, 1984). Indeed, the interest in the common factors approach has been labeled one of the most significant trends in psychotherapy (Bergin, 1982; Gurman, 1980).

Reconsideration of the Common Nonspecific Approach

Certain influences have contributed to the reconsideration of common nonspecific factors, including the increase in the number of different techniques, mounting evidence that in practice competing treatments overlap, data showing that treatment and "placebo" control conditions produce similar outcomes, and results from comparative studies, suggesting that competing treatments produce similar outcomes (Kazdin, 1986). The general lack of differences between the two psychotherapies in the NIMH study (which, as mentioned before, was the largest and most precise comparative study of psychotherapy ever undertaken) suggested to many researchers that a major effort should be put into studying the therapeutically active factors common to the different therapies (Elkin et al., 1989; Garfield and Bergin, 1986).

The common nonspecific approach provided researchers with a reasonable solution to the problem that emerged from the specific-approach findings, namely, that of "no differential effectiveness despite technical diversity" (Stiles, Shapiro, and Elliott, 1986, p. 165). Factors common to a variety of techniques provided researchers with a plausible explanation of the effects of diverse techniques. "If indeed the multitude of different psychotherapy systems can legitimately claim equal success, then perhaps they are not as diverse as they appear on the surface. They probably share certain core features; further, these common elements may be the curative elements—those responsible for therapeutic success, accounting for most of the gains resulting from psychological intervention" (Grencavage and Norcross, 1990, p. 372).

Common Factors Underlie Superficial Differences

Thus, according to the nonspecific approach, all therapies are effective—
and comparably effective—because they all wittingly or unwittingly share
the same therapeutic elements (also called factors, ingredients, or variables). These elements have been called nonspecific because they are common to all therapies. The idea of nonspecificity has been broadly interpreted as including everything that is not encompassed in the construct of
specificity. It has been used to refer to placebo and to common elements
such as the therapeutic alliance, suggestion, attention, empathy, and hope
(Elkin et al., 1989; Garfield and Bergin, 1986).

The common nonspecific approach proposes that a major limitation of
past studies is that they focused on characteristics unique to a specific treatment rather than on more general factors included in that treatment. According to this view, differences in theoretical constructs or clinical techniques are more superficial than real and may mask some basic underlying
similarities. Supporters of this approach argue that features common to
all therapies underlie or override differences in therapists' verbal techniques
and that these common features are responsible for the general equivalence
in effectiveness. In terms of the pharmacological analogy, the assumption
is that despite the superficial differences in color between red and blue pills
there is an equivalence of mechanism.

The common nonspecific approach proposes that a more useful way of
addressing the question of how therapy works is to search for the factors
that are common to all therapies. This view is based on the belief that these
factors may be at least as important in accounting for therapy outcome as
the unique factors that differentiate them. The common factors identified
may then become the basis for more parsimonious theory and technique
(Goldfried, 1980; Frank, 1961, 1982). The common nonspecific approach
seeks to find the active ingredients shared by the different therapies with
the eventual goal of developing more efficacious treatments based on
these ingredients.

The major goals of the nonspecific approach are to identify the ingredients that are common among alternative treatments and to discover the
profile of ingredients that are most strongly associated with positive therapeutic outcome. The findings, according to the common nonspecific viewpoint, may then have implications for eventually defining what effective
treatments need to include. The questions addressed by the common non-

specific approach are, "What factors are common across therapies? Do these factors account for treatment outcome?" The identification of common factors, with its promise of greater generality, are considered essential for demonstrating equivalence of mechanism across therapies.

Alternative Interpretations

The common factors approach has led to a variety of post hoc speculations about factors that may cut across therapies. Different positions have been advanced to suggest that the crucial ingredients of therapy are identical despite differences in technique.

For example, Frank (1961, 1978) has suggested that therapies produce their effects because they share the following features: (1) an emotionally charged and confiding relationship; (2) a setting in which the therapist's role as an expert is assumed; (3) an accepted explanation for the condition; and (4) a healing ritual promoting positive expectation and the reversal of demoralization. In this formulation, the specific content of various technical interventions (be they psychoanalysis, behavior therapy, or shamanism) is necessary to provide a shared belief system and the structure of the healing ritual but is not specifically or differentially effective in the way that their practitioners have assumed them to be. Shapiro (1971), expressing a similar view in different terms, suggested that the placebo effect shared by various forms of psychotherapy is more effective in promoting change than their presumed specific differences. In this formulation, the successes of different methods of psychotherapy are due to the elements that contribute to the placebo effect, including such elements as the patient-therapist relationship and patient suggestibility.

Other authors have sought to encompass all successful therapies within a common theoretical framework. For instance, Ryle (1978, 1982, 1984), in his procedural sequence model, suggested locating the different schools of psychotherapy within a more general cognitive theory. Orlinsky and Howard (1986), in their generic model of psychotherapy, proposed several components of the therapeutic process that they view as active in any therapy (the therapeutic contract, therapeutic interventions, the therapeutic bond, patient self-relatedness, and therapeutic realizations) and discussed their social, cultural, and psychological aspects and implications. Other interpretations of psychotherapy have included self-efficacy theory (Bandura, 1977), personal construct theory (Leitner, 1982), and intergrationism (Goldfried, 1982). These, too, have suggested that the features common among different treatments are responsible for producing therapeutic change.

Other proponents of the common nonspecific approach have advocated stage or phase models that have a variety of change mechanisms coming into play at different times. Thus, Prochaska and DiClemente (1986) have proposed a stage theory of change and described five stages of change (precontemplation, contemplation, decision making, action, and maintenance) that interact with basic change mechanisms such as catharsis and reinforcement. Urban and Ford (1971) have characterized all therapies as forms of problem solving following five stages. Howard et al. (1993) have proposed a three-phase model of psychotherapeutic change including remoralization, remediation, and rehabilitation and have suggested that certain classes of interventions are appropriate for different phases of therapy.

Broad Commonalities

Apart from theoretical excursions, empirical studies have suggested that some broad commonalities exist in diverse therapies. Typically the commonalities were studied independently of treatment efficacy. For instance, in studies that merely ask clients what was helpful to them, clients tend to emphasize the importance of the therapist rather than specific technical interventions or interpretations (Strupp, Fox, and Lessler, 1969). In an uncontrolled follow-up study of 112 patients whom he had seen in his behaviorally oriented practice, Lazarus (1971) asked patients to provide their perceptions of what was effective. Patients thought the personal qualities of the therapist were more important than specific technical factors. They used such adjectives as "sensitive," "honest," and "gentle" to describe desirable therapist characteristics.

Other studies have shown that such general characteristics as therapist empathy and the use of interpretative and clarifying statements are similar among such seemingly diverse techniques as Gestalt therapy, psychodynamic therapy, and behavior therapy (Brunik and Schroeder, 1979; Sloane et al., 1975). In the Sloane et al. study, behavior therapists and psychotherapists were rated similarly on such characteristics as warmth and positive regard, and behavior therapists showed significantly higher levels of accurate empathy and interpersonal contact. The generality of the conclusions can be seriously questioned given the small number of psychotherapists (n = 3) and behavior therapists (n = 3). However, the findings suggested to many researchers that differences in discussions about alternative therapies may be blurred in the actual practice of the treatments (Kazdin, 1986). Other studies also have shown that the general therapist attribute "giving support," which was supposed to be especially characteristic of supportive, psychodynamically oriented therapy, also was present in different treatments including drug counseling and cognitive behavioral therapy (Luborsky et al., 1982).

Broad Commonalities and Outcome

An important goal of the common factors approach has been the demonstration that a common process factor is related to outcome. Typically, the search for the common factor-outcome link fell into broad domains of therapist characteristics and client characteristics (Stiles, Shapiro, and Elliott, 1986). Under therapist characteristics the general category of positive descriptors (personal warmth, trustworthiness, empathy, genuineness) has yielded mixed results. These positive therapist attributes were initially accepted by researchers and hailed as common ingredients that predict therapeutic benefit. However, later reviews have shown inconclusive results (Chinsky and Rappaport, 1970; Gormally and Hill, 1974; Lambert, DeJulio, and Stein, 1978; Mitchell, Bozarth, and Krauft, 1977; Parloff, Waskow, and Wolfe, 1978; Shapiro, 1976).

Another group of studies focused on client characteristics during treatment. Under client characteristics some general categories of client involvement (client exploration, client expectancies, depth of experiencing, patient participation, positive contributions) have yielded somewhat more consistent evidence. The research has suggested that global measures such as the overall level of patient participation, positive contributions, or the total number of patient utterances in therapy predict improvement at the end of treatment. That is, studies have shown that outcome is optimized when patients actively collaborate in the therapeutic process. However, although the client's participation is related to outcome, there remains ambiguity about which specific aspects of that role are crucial (Stiles, Shapiro, and Elliott, 1986).

Summary of Results

In general, studies attempting to associate patient or therapist characteristics with therapeutic outcome have been disappointing. Reviews of studies in this area have yielded only low to moderate correlations of therapists' factors and outcome variables (for comprehensive reviews, see Lambert,

Shapiro, and Bergin, 1986; Orlinsky and Howard, 1986; Parloff, Waskow, and Wolfe, 1978; Schaffer, 1982). In a recent meta-analytic critique of process-outcome research, the findings show that process-outcome studies have not yielded strong evidence for the efficacy of therapist interventions (Shapiro et al., 1994). The overall effect size was 0.26. "This would be equivalent to a correlation of about .13, and the intervention would account for a little under 2% of the variance in outcomes. The clinical importance of an effect of this magnitude is, of course, questionable" (Shapiro et al., 1994, p. 27). The results of the meta-analysis reveal how little empirical knowledge we have of effective psychotherapeutic techniques.

The difficulties of specifying and measuring global, value-laden therapist characteristics contribute much to the weak showing. Despite extensive research on therapists' contributions to psychotherapy, little progress has been made in understanding or empirically demonstrating how the therapist contributes to the success or failure of psychotherapy. "Many reviews have suggested that this lack of progress is due to (a) inadequate conceptualizations of how therapist interventions impact patients and (b) methods of evaluating therapist behaviors that are too global, imprecise, or clinically irrelevant" (Silberschatz and Curtis, 1993, p. 403). In a related critique, Orlinsky and Howard (1978), recognizing the progress in prediction of outcome by patient process variables, expressed concern that univariate prediction is useful knowledge but falls short of the desired conclusions that certain features of the process produce good or poor outcomes. Other authors have claimed that the prevalence of simplifying assumptions about therapy process research has produced quantitative results, which are not useful to therapists (Elliott and Anderson, 1994). Examples of some simplifying assumptions are "one type of variable is enough," "all therapy events are equally important," "patterns are not important," and "only one thing happens at a time" (Elliott and Anderson, 1994, p. 69).

Thus, despite the centrality of the above findings to our awareness of the importance of patients' and therapists' characteristics and treatment outcomes, current research methods have not provided specific descriptions of the therapeutic process. Much of the inconclusiveness can be traced to difficulties in measuring relevant components of the therapeutic process. The usual rating procedures have been criticized as providing only global evaluations, which say little about the specifics of the therapeutic process (Stiles, Shapiro, and Elliott, 1986). Researchers have concluded that the conventional process-outcome analysis is inadequate for revealing how therapy works.

THE THERAPEUTIC ALLIANCE AS THE COMMON INGREDIENT

The earlier hope of finding a common ingredient in the therapists' characteristics or patients' characteristics appears to have been replaced by the hope of finding a common ingredient in the relationship between therapist and client. In the search for effective ingredients common to all psychotherapies, researchers have identified the *therapeutic alliance* (also called *helping alliance* or *working alliance*) as a central aspect of the patient-therapist relationship. Of the common factors investigated in psychotherapy, none has received more attention and confirmation than the importance of the therapeutic alliance. Researchers believe the success of any therapeutic quest depends on the participants' establishing an open, trusting, collaborative relationship—the therapeutic alliance. Given that work on the therapeutic alliance has been highly influential, we will review it here in some detail.

The Idea of the Therapeutic Alliance

The influence of the therapist-client relationship on the outcome of psychotherapy is an old theme in the psychotherapy literature. The idea of the therapeutic alliance originated in the psychoanalytic literature, and it is there that most discussion of it can be found. As early as 1895, Breuer and Freud spoke of the patient as an active collaborator in treatment. In most of his later work on the psychoanalytic relationship, Freud focused on transference and resistance. He explored the difference between the neurotic aspects of the client's attachment to the analyst (transference) and the friendly and positive feelings the client has toward the therapist. He felt that the positive, reality-based aspect of the relationship provided the basis for a therapeutic partnership against the common enemy, the client's neurosis. Freud described the analyst and patient as banding together against the patient's symptoms in a "pact" based on free exploration by the patient and discretion and competent understanding by the therapist.

In Freud's view, the patient's collaboration was fostered by two sources—rapport and the technical activity of the analyst. Rapport was a transference development based on earlier affectionate and helping relationships (Freud, 1912/1966, 1913/1966). Freud, however, also recognized the role of friendliness and affection as "the vehicle of success in psychoanalysis" (1912/1966, p. 105). "The technical activity of the analyst—his or her careful handling of resistances, avoidance of hasty interpretations, and avoidance of moralizing or taking sides in the patient's conflicts—was considered by Freud to be most important in developing proper rapport. Without such developments the patient would not listen to, accept, or work with the therapist to understand and interpret his or her difficulties" (Frieswyk et al., 1986, pp. 32–33).

Beginning with Zetzel (1956), psychoanalytically oriented therapists paid increasing attention to the notion that the therapeutic alliance, which depends on the patient's basic trust and on the therapist's active participation, is essential to the effectiveness of any therapeutic intervention. Yet within the psychoanalytic/psychodynamic approach there is ample controversy concerning the nature of the idea. There is, for instance, disagreement whether therapist activity should be included as a component of the therapeutic alliance and whether the therapeutic alliance is part of transference or distinct from it.

According to Bordin (1976), for example, the therapeutic alliance depends on the work that the therapist and patient do together. He conceptualizes the alliance as including the patient's underlying attitudes and experiences (for example, trust and attachment) with the patient's collaboration in the tasks of therapy. In contrast, other authors (Frieswyk et al., 1986) define the therapeutic alliance solely as a patient variable and separate the alliance from various aspects of the patient's experience of the relationship. They argue that the therapeutic alliance should be conceptualized strictly as the patient's collaboration in the tasks of psychotherapy. They distinguish the alliance from various aspects of the patient's experience (especially transference) and separate alliance from issues of technique.

The Importance of the Therapeutic Relationship

Although the idea of the therapeutic alliance is not discussed by theorists of other approaches, most schools of therapy focus on relationship issues. The therapeutic relationship's importance is recognized, for instance, in interpersonal therapy and even in cognitive therapy, behavior therapy, and strategic family therapies. Cognitive therapists are advised to watch for relationship issues and make them explicit when they happen in treatment (Beck, 1978). Beck suggests using warmth, confidence, and enthusiasm to establish a constructive relationship, adding that the exact mix of these factors will vary according to the particular therapist-patient pair.

Also, family therapists are advised to be less "strategic," "manipulative," and "instrumental" and more "collaborative," "flexible," "empathic," and "validating." These qualities are thought to refine a strategic family therapist's relationship skills and improve his or her ability to facilitate a patient's progress in therapy (Duncan, 1992; Hoffman, 1985). Although the term *therapeutic alliance* is not used in behavior therapy there also has been a long-standing discussion among behaviorists regarding the role of the therapist-client relationship in determining outcome. Many behaviorists (for example, Goldstein, Heller, and Sechrest, 1966) claim the relationship between therapist and client is a critical factor in treatment. Citing evidence that verbal conditioning influences opinions, attitudes, and personality changes, some authors consider the behavior therapist as a social reinforcer and place the therapeutic relationship within a social learning context (Wilson, Hannon, and Evans, 1968).

Retrospective accounts by former clients (Cross, Sheehan, and Kahan, 1982; Feifel and Eelles, 1963; Llewelyn and Hume, 1979) typically describe relationship qualities such as support and understanding as the most helpful factors. These reports have also been construed as measuring the importance of the therapeutic alliance (Stiles, Shapiro, and Elliott, 1986).

The Therapeutic Alliance as a Generic Concept

Noting that the therapeutic relationship is relevant across a broad range of therapies, several clinicians and researchers, largely identified with time-limited dynamic psychotherapy, have reconceptualized the therapeutic alliance as a generic concept (Bordin, 1975, 1976; Hartley, 1985). According to the generic view, competent therapists of all persuasions can form a positive emotional bond and a sense of mutual collaboration with receptive clients, and this relationship carries most of the therapeutic weight.

The generic view of the alliance implies that there is an interaction between relationship factors and technique (Hartley and Strupp, 1983; Docherty, 1985). In contrast to those theorists who argue for the superiority of relationship versus technical factors in influencing outcome, according to Docherty (1985) the development of a good therapeutic alliance within any method is related to the skillful application of psychotherapeutic techniques. That is, in contrast to the view that the therapeutic bond between therapist and patient must be fostered as a prerequisite to effective treatment, the generic view implies that neither the alliance nor technical intervention precedes or follows the other.

The goal of most of the research has been to design a method that could be applied across a broad range of therapies (Hartley, 1985). This aim seems to signify that most investigators now working in this area regard the therapeutic alliance as a generic component of the therapist-patient relationship that can be measured in different types of treatments (Krupnick, 1988). Despite the claim of the broad utility of the therapeutic alliance concept, the development of instruments has thus far been psychodynamic in conceptualization.

Alliance Scales

About six different observer-rated instruments have been created to assess the therapeutic alliance—the Penn Helping Alliance Method, the Toronto Therapeutic Alliance Scale, the California Psychotherapy Alliance Scale, the Vanderbilt Therapeutic Alliance Scale, the Working Alliance Inventory, and the Vanderbilt Psychotherapy Process Scale. (Unlike the other instruments, the Vanderbilt Psychotherapy Process Scale was not specifically designed to serve as a measure of the therapeutic alliance. However, it includes some conceptual components that overlap with the therapeutic alliance.)

Each of these measures arose from a somewhat different definition of the alliance, its role in therapy, and the most appropriate source (client or therapist). The definitions of the alliance used by the various authors (for example, Gomes-Schwartz, 1978; Hartley, 1985; Horowitz and Marmar, 1985; Horvath and Greenberg, 1989; Luborsky, 1976; Marmar, Weiss, and Gaston, 1989; Marziali, 1984; Strupp and Hadley, 1979) suggest, however, that the ideas of collaboration, mutuality, and engagement are the strong common elements among all representations of this construct. Also, accumulating evidence suggests that the intercorrelation among these measures is substantial (Hansell, 1990; Saburin et al., 1990; Tichenor and Hill, 1989). And strong intercorrelations between these instruments were documented at the subscale level (Bachelor, 1990; Hansell, 1990).

Global Rating Methods

All the existing alliance scales are aimed at measuring the post hoc level of the overall alliance or the level of patients' and therapists' separate contributions to the alliance. Typically, clinical judges read excerpts of therapy transcripts and rate the number of times particular positive or negative items occur. Items are selected based on consensual agreement that the items reflect the theoretical construct. For instance, judges are asked to rate whether a therapist is actively attentive, pursuing leads in the patient's productions, applying his skills in the patient's interest. Qualities in the negative direction on this item include indifference, withdrawal, passivity, or an attitude of "just doing a job." Items such as these are based on the consensual notion that they are an important component of the therapeutic alliance construct.

Other alliance scales ask clients or therapists to rate their perception of the therapeutic alliance. Typically a client or therapist is asked to rate the degree to which particular statements accurately reference his or her experience in the current therapy situation on a 5-point "Likert" scale (1—never; 2—seldom; 3—sometimes; 4—often; 5—always). For instance, a client or therapist is asked to rate the degree to which the goals established in the therapy relationship are shared and accepted or whether therapist and client experience a sense of mutual trust, liking, understanding, and caring. It is assumed, based on consensual agreement, that items such as "shared goals" and "a sense of mutual caring" are essential components for forming an effective therapeutic alliance (Horvath and Greenberg, 1986).

The alliance scales are essentially *global* methods that use *frequency counts* for rating the presence or absence of *unidimensional* and *static variables*. The alliance scales represent researchers' attempts to translate the therapeutic alliance construct into items. The items are generally unidimensional, unconditional, static characteristics of the therapist, the client, and their relationship. It is assumed that a positively defined item ("caring," "actively attentive," and so on) that occurs frequently will produce a better alliance, which is essential for success in therapy.

Summary of Results

These methods for quantifying the alliance opened the way to the empirical exploration of the relation of the alliance and therapy outcome. Current research includes studies of the impact of the alliance in psychodynamic, cognitive, and experiential therapy (for example, Greenberg and Webster, 1982; Luborsky, 1976; Rounsaville et al., 1987) across a wide range of client problems and outcomes (for example, Frank and Gunderson, 1990; Gomes-Schwartz, 1978; Horvath and Greenberg, 1989). The effect of the alliance has been examined in both short- and longer-term interventions (Frank and Gunderson, 1990; Kokotovic and Tracey, 1990) and from the client's, the therapist's, and independent observers' perspectives (Marziali, 1984; Tichenor and Hill, 1989).

The data show that the therapeutic alliance is associated with outcomes whatever the therapy approach employed. These results are consistent across different types of outcome measures and different sources of information (client, therapist, or clinical judge). It is widely acclaimed that the therapeutic alliance is the most robust predictor of outcome. Proponents of this view have hailed it as the most promising process variable. A recent meta-analysis has confirmed the finding that a positive therapeutic alliance is associated with good therapy outcome; however, the overall effect size (0.26) is not very large (Horvath and Symonds, 1991). The authors state: "Although the effect size is not very large, it is within the range of values reported for other important psychotherapy variables" (p. 146). Interestingly, what these authors label as "important" others have interpreted as unimportant. In the meta-analytic critique of process-outcome research mentioned before (Shapiro et al., 1994), the overall effect size was also 0.26. However, these authors concluded that the importance and clinical significance of an effect of this magnitude are questionable.

Besides the issue of whether an effect size of this magnitude is important, other issues have been raised to dampen the current enthusiasm for the therapeutic alliance concept. In some respects, researchers say, the existing research has posed more questions that it has answered. "First, correlations with outcome may in fact reflect confounding with early outcome. Early success or partial symptom relief is likely to strengthen the therapeutic alliance so that the relationship to outcome may be bidirectional" (Stiles, Shapiro, and Elliott, 1986, p. 174). Second, despite the growing body of evidence to support the importance of the therapeutic alliance as a predictor of outcome, there has been little emphasis on identifying and validating the specific components of this complex construct.

RELEVANCE OF THE THERAPEUTIC ALLIANCE
TO THE PRACTICE OF PSYCHOTHERAPY

The finding that alliance variables have robust correlations with outcome still leaves considerable uncertainty about precisely what it is that various alliance systems measure. "Most psychotherapists have not found the therapeutic alliance construct sufficient for assessing the effectiveness of their techniques or for explaining how patients change; it locates the common core at too high a level of abstraction" (Jones and Pulos, 1993, p. 306). Researchers and clinicians have pointed out that the findings merely suggest that some global relationship factor may be recognizable but not easily operationalized. Existing instruments rate the general relationship climate with items such as "attentive" and "caring." Although such methods have provided useful descriptive accounts that serve in a general sense to distinguish good from poor relationships, they do not specify what the therapist *does* to establish the quality of the relationship. Global methods thus may encourage the view that the relationship is just a generic factor unrelated to specific therapeutic actions. Also, the fallacy in studies that rate process on single variables is that all client or therapist behaviors receiving the same rating on a single item (such as "caring" or "actively attentive") are assumed to have the same therapeutic significance and the same effect on outcome (Greenberg, 1986). Several writers have pointed out that frequency counts ignore the sequential nature of the therapeutic process (Greenberg, 1986; Gottman, Markman, and Notarius 1977). These writers suggest that it is more the occurrence of a *pattern of variables* than their frequency of occurrence that should be the target of study.

Clinical inferences drawn from studies on the alliance are similar to the instruments used. They are essentially global, static, and unidimensional. For instance, as mentioned before, therapists are advised to be less "strategic," "manipulative," and "instrumental" and more "collaborative," "flexible," "empathic," and "validating." These qualities are thought to refine family therapists' relationship skills and improve their ability to facilitate a patient's progress in therapy (Duncan, 1992; Heatherington, 1990; Hoffman, 1985). They say nothing, however, about what a therapist should *do* during the moment-to moment changes in the patient-therapist relationship. It is easy to suggest that a competent therapist should establish a good therapeutic alliance or be more empathetic and validating with a patient, but it is much more difficult to define precisely which therapist actions will best achieve such a goal.

To sum up, research on the therapeutic alliance has produced some important findings. Among these are the discoveries that it is possible to quantify this variable and that it is possible for judges to rate the construct reliably. Scales that have been developed for this purpose have been shown to demonstrate adequate reliability. Almost all reviewers think the therapist-patient relationship is critical; however, they point out that research support for this position is more ambiguous than once was the case. The findings are clearly important for highlighting the association between a relationship factor and outcome. Yet, the findings do not provide precise descriptions of participant actions intrinsic to the relationship factor.

One cannot use such data as a basis for drawing conclusions about which specific patient and therapist actions will maximize a good therapeutic alliance. In other words, the findings do not shed light on the inner workings of the therapeutic relationship: "the alliance construct is really only a conceptual umbrella for uniting a number of client and therapist contributions; the exact operation of these constituent factors remains to be clarified" (Stiles, Shapiro, and Elliott, 1986, p. 174). Thus, we still do not know how relationship factors operate in the actions of the participants, what they reflect, or why they predict outcome. In short, the link between relationship factors and treatment outcome is not in itself a description of how therapy works; it is a relation in search of an explanation.

Researchers agree that a crucial issue in psychotherapy research thus concerns developing a measure that specifies what the participants do to establish a therapeutic relationship. "What is required, in fact, is an investigation strategy of discovery that evaluates the therapeutic change events microscopically" (Frieswyk et al., 1986, p. 36). More specifically, a method is needed that can describe and measure aspects of patients' actions that shift or remain stable during treatment and measure aspects of therapists' actions that facilitate or impede progress in therapy. A method that can describe in-therapy performance will enable reliable description of the therapeutic relationship at a level of clinical relevance. There is a growing conviction among psychotherapy researchers that the first goal of research should be the development of a system to further a more comprehensive description of the therapeutic process (Greenberg, 1986). An operational research language that is not theoretically specific and that uses everyday English is needed to carry out the kind of process-outcome research that will permit comparisons across therapies (Wolfe and Goldfried, 1988). This operational approach to the definition of practice of psychotherapy must be flexible enough to permit the clinician both spontaneity and necessary therapeutic improvisation.

Summing Up

Although we know that psychotherapy works, we do not clearly understand how it works. Despite differences in therapists' techniques and theories, most reviews of psychotherapy outcome research show little or no differential effectiveness of different psychotherapies. That is to say, differently labeled therapies have demonstrably different behavioral contents yet appear to have equivalent outcomes.

This finding presents a problem to researchers and practitioners. The findings of outcome equivalence and technical nonequivalence present a problem because they seem to imply that no matter what theory a therapist espouses, the result is the same.

Two possible approaches have appeared to resolve this issue. The unique specific approach argues, mainly on methodological grounds, that therapies may, after all, differ in outcome. This approach challenges the apparent equivalence of outcome, arguing that differential results could be revealed by more sensitive reviewing procedures. An important development in this approach is the use of treatment manuals. Proponents of this approach feel that a major advantage of treatment manuals is that they standardize the delivery of treatment and allow researchers a method of sorting out the common factors from the unique factors associated with specific treatment approaches. The development and use of treatment manuals by the NIMH Depression Collaborative Study illustrates the use of manuals in psychotherapy research. The results of this research show, however, that increasing the standardization of treatment does not result in clearer evidence regarding the relative effectiveness of alternative techniques among the treatments for less severely depressed patients.

Also, several authors have pointed out the drawbacks of using manuals to train therapists to participate in psychotherapy outcome studies (Weissman, Rounsaville, and Chevron, 1982; Rounsaville et al., 1986). The move toward improved methodology raises critical questions regarding the issue of clinical relevance. Techniques included in manuals may differ from those that are used in practice. The results of studies using manuals are obviously important, but they do not necessarily reflect what happens in clinical practice. Everyone who has tried to learn how to play tennis or write a story from a book knows how difficult it can be to act from such a description, for there are many other factors to consider in practice that are left out of guidebooks. There always is a gap between such descriptions and the reality to which they refer (Schön, 1983, p. 276). Rules of an art can be useful, but they do not determine the practice of an art; they can serve as a guide only if they can be integrated into the practical knowledge of doing the art (Polanyi, 1958).

It is not surprising, then, that when training therapists to follow the rules of a manual certain problems appeared. Some therapists were simply unable to follow the manual consistently (Rounsaville et al., 1986). Therapists who were bound to a particular psychotherapeutic approach that was different from the procedures of the manual had difficulty using the manual (Weissman, Rounsaville, and Chevron, 1982). Other therapists followed the manual in a too-rigid, cookbook fashion. "Rigidly proceeding down the list of suggested initial questions, rather than sensitively eliciting the patient's view of his or her problem, worked against a key feature of treatment, the development of an empathic therapeutic alliance" (Weissman, Rounsaville, and Chevron, 1982, p. 1444). It is as though the therapist found himself or herself with two different sets of information—on one hand, the dynamics of the human situation, and on the other, specific treatment rules of the therapeutic encounter. Although manuals are useful for standardizing theoretical ideas thought to be relevant to a particular treatment, it appears they are not very useful for training therapists to understand the dynamics of how therapy actually is practiced.

In contrast to the unique specific approach, the common nonspecific approach argues, mainly on conceptual grounds, that despite superficial diversity of content, the core ingredients or mechanisms are the same across therapies. This approach challenges the seeming differences among treatments, arguing that a higher-order theory or a higher-order common process factor can encompass superficial diversity. Several different theories and factors have been proposed to be of a higher order. Besides theoretical speculations, an important goal of the common factors approach is the demonstration that a common process factor is related to outcome.

The therapeutic alliance probably is the quintessential common variable because its importance does not lie within the specifications of one school of thought. It is now commonly accepted by most orientations that the therapeutic relationship is of essential importance to the conduct of psychotherapy. Although attempting to be inclusive, the alliance is an abstract idea that does not specify the dynamic, interactive influence of therapist and client. We still do not know how relationship factors operate in the actions of the participants. Thus, there is still a need to define what participants *do* to establish a therapeutic relationship.

There is a growing consensus in the field that what is needed is an operational approach to the definition of the practice of psychotherapy. The approach must be precise enough to specify what the ingredients of psychotherapy are and flexible enough to describe the different ways that psychotherapy is practiced. It must be based on what therapists and patients do, that is to say, on their actions during the therapeutic encounter. This feature can help narrow the gap between research and clinical practice.

"The important question in thinking about the relation between the work psychotherapists do and the knowledge that research can provide them is, Upon what knowledge do they actually draw as they do psychotherapy?" (Edelson, 1994, p. 65). In other words, what is the kind of knowing in which expert clinicians engage? And how is clinical knowing like and unlike the kind of knowledge presented in theories of psychotherapy (research-based knowledge)? We shall explore these issues next when we examine the modes of thinking underlying knowing-in-theory and knowing-in-practice.

2

Two Types of Knowledge

Theory and Practice

Heinz von Foerster used to tell the story of a conversation he had with his uncle, Ludwig Wittgenstein, while growing up in Vienna. Wittgenstein asked the boy what he wanted to be when he grew up. "I want to be a natural scientist," the young Foerster said. The uncle replied, "You will have to learn many, many things to be a natural scientist." "But, I know them already," insisted the boy. "Ah," said the uncle, "but you will have to study very much to learn what you know."

KNOWING-IN-THEORY AND KNOWING-IN-PRACTICE

The story shows that there are at least two kinds of knowledge. One kind is explicit, learned, and deliberate; the other kind is tacit, spontaneous, and automatic. We might call the first way of knowledge *knowing-in-theory* and the second way *knowing-in-practice*. This is not, of course, an unfamiliar dichotomy (Barnard, 1936/1964; Bruner, 1986; Giacomo and Weissmark, 1986, 1987; Polanyi, 1958; Simon, 1983). These two different ways of knowing feed into the familiar division between the "hard" knowledge of science and research and the "soft" knowledge of artistry and practice.

The discussion between the practitioner and the researcher reflects the division between these two ways of knowing. The practitioner argues therapy is effective because his experience tells him so. He says that he derives little guidance from the scientific literature because it does not address the questions he is most interested in. Psychotherapy research, he asserts, is interested in big, general questions. But he, the practitioner, is more interested in a particular patient (Edelson, 1994; Havens, 1994). The practitioner claims that doing psychotherapy is a work of unique particulars, not generalities. He explains that doing psychotherapy involves dealing with the here and now, with situations of indeterminacy, instability, uniqueness, and value conflict.

The researcher counters that the practitioner naively trusts his observations and intuitions. She argues that practitioners, in general, are not rigorous enough. She insists that if therapy is an effective method of treatment then some of its components, or some global measure of the process, should be measurable.

The practitioner counters that the researcher is missing the point. The problem, he says, is not whether practitioners should rely on "hard," measurable facts or "soft" intuitions. The real problem, he says, is in discovering what the expert practitioner knows how to do well—therapy. Experts' knowledge is clinically useful, the practitioner says, and can teach researchers a lot. If one wishes to study the psychology of mathematics, the practitioner says, one studies the works of trained and gifted mathematicians, with emphasis on the heuristics and the formalisms they use to give form to their mathematical intuitions. Likewise, one does well to study the work of expert therapists if one is to understand what it is that competent therapists actually do.

The researcher admits that more work needs to be done on what it is that expert therapists do in practice. Part of the problem, the researcher explains, is that although most professionals recognize "good" therapists when they see them, research has been slow to define and operationalize excellence in a systematic way. The problem is, the researcher says, that knowing-in-practice has, to date, remained unspecifiable. Yet, it is the very heart of a science of psychotherapy.

In the end, both the practitioner and the researcher agree that an approach to psychotherapy research that captures the process of knowing-in-practice would generate clinically useful knowledge.

The difficulty of specifying what it is that expert therapists actually do is not a new problem. Freud recognized it as early as 1904. Although Freud obviously was skillful at doing the psychotherapy techniques he developed, he felt uneasy because he could not describe what he knew how to do. He could not justify its quality or rigor. Freud realized that this inability to specify his knowledge-in-practice left the method vulnerable to the claim that it was not a legitimate form of professional knowing.

When giving a lecture about hysteria to his colleagues, Freud said that he was glad his theory of hysteria was widely accepted, but it was unfortunate that his psychotherapy method was not equally recognized. He said to his colleagues, "It was impossible for me to give medical readers the directions necessary to enable them to carry through the method of psychotherapy treatment. . . . To many physicians, psychotherapy seems to be the offspring of modern mysticism and, compared with our physico-chemical specifics which are applied on the basis of physiological knowledge, psychotherapy appears quite unscientific and unworthy of the attention of a serious investigator" (Freud 1904/1959, p. 250).

The situation has not changed much since Freud's time. There is an "inconsistency between the clinicians' day-to-day observations regarding the apparent utility of their efforts and the researchers' failure to furnish enthusiastic confirmation" (Parloff and Dies, 1977, p. 312). This inconsistency has contributed to a widening gap between theory and action, research and practice.

Today researchers and clinicians recognize that research-based knowledge is different from the knowledge practitioners use in the midst of action. Although clinicians sometimes make use of theories and techniques, in much of the spontaneous behavior of practice they depend on tacit recognitions and clinical judgments.

Consider an analogy: riding a bicycle. There is a theoretical rule of bicycle riding that states that for a given angle of unbalance the curvature of each winding is inversely proportional to the square of the speed at which the cyclist is proceeding. "But does this tell us exactly how to ride a bicycle? No. You obviously cannot adjust the curvature of your bicycle's path in proportion to the ratio of your unbalance over the square of your speed; and if you could you would fall off the machine, for there are a number of other factors to be taken into account in practice which are left out in the formulation of this rule" (Polanyi, 1958, p. 50).

Similarly, situations of clinical practice are characterized by unique factors that cannot be predicted before treatment takes place. To the extent that the spontaneity of the therapist's actions is considered crucial, it is evident that theory-based knowledge does not describe or account for the clinical competence that practitioners sometimes reveal in what they do.

Adherence versus Competence

The distinction between theory-based knowledge and clinical competence was recognized in the NIMH Collaborative Research Program. With the trend toward developing manuals came an interest in measuring the extent to which therapists do what is prescribed in the manuals. The assumption was that therapists must *adhere* to the treatment at some minimum level before it can be supposed that the intended treatment was offered. A distinction was made, however, between *adherence*, which refers to how much therapists use techniques considered appropriate to their treatment approach, and *competence,* which refers to how skillfully or adequately they apply the techniques (Hill, O'Grady, and Elkin, 1992).

Implicit in this distinction between adherence and competence is the recognition that therapists' expertise also depends on *clinical judgment* of situations, or *practical knowledge.* In other words, the construct of competence refers to aspects of the delivery of treatment such as appropriate timing, quality of the intervention, and depth of interpretation (Hill, O'Grady, and Elkin, 1992). Researchers realized that although much attention was paid to the careful definition of the treatment interventions, one additional component that should be included in the definition and in the interpretation of the effects of an intervention is how competently the therapists actually carry out the treatment (Elkin, 1994). Carrying out the treatment depends on the context, the patient, and on the ability of a particular therapist. The therapists' use of procedures may vary enormously in competence, which could include such hard-to-specify aspects of technique as choosing the appropriate depth of interpretation, the proper within-session context for interventions, and other therapeutic behaviors that occur over the course of treatment.

As mentioned before, the arguments for specifying studied treatments via manualization are compelling. The manual represents an effort to operationalize, to the extent possible, intervention techniques that constitute "the doing" of therapy according to a particular theoretical approach. Yet researchers recognize that manuals do not reflect all that occurs within treatment or the sessions any more than a "map is the terrain" (Kazdin, 1994). Although manuals are useful for specifying and prescribing types of interventions, they cannot determine how a particular therapist will deliver the intervention. Manuals cannot prescribe a therapist's idiosyncratic interpretation of treatment techniques. The evidence of how a specific treatment was delivered can be found only in the records of the actual treatment.

What a therapist does in treatment depends on what is happening. Here we enter the realm of clinical judgment, which cannot be standardized before treatment takes place. Any therapeutic encounter is necessarily typified by improvisations. Experts' knowledge always is dynamic and promotes context-dependent understanding, whereas manuals are acontextual (Giacomo and Weissmark, 1986, 1987). Manuals can specify the components of a treatment, but they cannot sequence or prioritize those components.

Because situations of practice are characterized by unique and unpredictable events, it is not possible to prioritize the components of a treatment before the treatment takes place.

Adherence to the rules in a manual can limit therapists' flexibility to deal with the dynamic and unpredictable events that occur in practice. The guidelines in a manual are unconditional, but events in therapy are dependent on the situation. Manuals, for instance, cannot prescribe how a particular patient will respond to an intervention. "Thus, a balance must be maintained between following the specified procedures and adapting the treatment to the needs of each patient. If the guidelines are followed in an overly rigid, 'cookbook' fashion, spontaneous development of a helping alliance can be undermined" (Weissman, Rounsaville, and Chevron, 1982, p. 1444).

Today, proponents of the specific approach suggest that adherence to a treatment approach may be less efficacious than allowing therapists to use their clinical judgment about which techniques to administer given their perceptions of patient needs. In addition, they recommend that research be conducted to decide whether treatment outcome is related to competence or to what therapists do at specific moments within therapy (Elkin, 1994). Researchers thus recognize that competent practitioners exhibit a kind of knowing-in-practice that is unlike the kind of knowledge in manuals and cannot be measured by the extent to which therapists do (adhere to) what is prescribed in a manual.

Skillful Ability

Proponents of the common approach also recognize that theory-based knowledge is different from the knowledge practitioners use in practice. As mentioned before, these researchers are interested in showing that a common process factor is related to outcome. According to this view, the different theories of psychotherapy mask underlying similarities. The similarities are thought to be at the level of practice common to all therapies. For instance, the therapeutic alliance factor is thought to be common to all therapies and is constituted in part by the doing of specific things in therapy that seem to make a difference (Greenberg and Pinsof, 1986). That is to say, the development of a good therapeutic alliance depends on the skillful ability of a therapist to form a collaborative relationship with a client. This implies that the *technical skill* of a therapist is a critical element for determining the outcome of treatment. Still, findings from alliance-related work have not shed any light on defining the technical factors that mark the skillful ability of a therapist. One cannot use the data as a basis for drawing conclusions about which specific therapist actions will maximize a collaborative relationship with a client. The exact operation of the therapist's contributions to the alliance remains to be clarified. As pointed out earlier, this may be due in part to the selection for study of overly simplistic global therapist variables such as mutual trust, shared goals, and a sense of caring. Such variables do not specify therapist activities that facilitate or impede alliance development.

Clinical Experience

Many practitioners, like researchers, believe that clinical knowledge is unlike the kind of knowledge presented in manuals, scientific papers, and books. "We also know that we have learned far more about how to do therapy from descriptive accounts (by writers, supervisors, and clients) than from the quantitative results of psychotherapy research" (Elliott and Anderson, 1994, p. 65). Practitioners have concluded that the practice of doing psychotherapy does not have much to do with science, scientific findings, or technical knowledge. "The very observations psychotherapy research selects, what it regards as an observation, and how it describes its observations are determined by its interest in the general. And so the observations it considers relevant are different from the observations the psychotherapist, who is inquiring into here-and-now particulars, finds relevant" (Edelson, 1994, p. 61).

Practitioners feel there is little to guide them through the uncertain, unique, and conflicted events of practice. Psychotherapy research, they claim, is interested in general predictions, in explanatory laws. But psychotherapists are interested in explanation, in making sense out of a particular case, and in making appropriate interventions. Knowledge derived from research simply does not help practitioners as they practice psychotherapy because it does not help them decide which interventions to make. Practitioners believe, therefore, that they have to rely on their clinical, intuitive experience as their main source of knowledge (Edelson, 1994).

What is clinical, intuitive experience all about? An experienced practitioner is one who confronts certain types of situations repeatedly. This is suggested by the way practitioners use the word *case*. The term suggests types of family-resembling situations (Polanyi, 1958; Simon, 1983). Practitioners become experts by experiencing many variations of a given situation and by developing a repertoire of patterns to recognize and to respond to these situations (Giacomo and Weissmark, 1986, 1987).

"Every professional entomologist," for instance, "has a comparable ability to discriminate among the insects he sees, and every botanist among the plants" (Simon, 1983, p. 26). Other examples include judgments of distance in golf or ball-throwing, or an experienced accountant who can look at a complex balance sheet and within seconds get a significant set of facts from it (Barnard, 1936/1968). "These facts do not leap from the paper and strike the eye. They lie between the figures in the part filled by the mind out of years of experience and technical knowledge. This is what makes out of a set of figures something to which then reason can usefully be applied. These non-logical processes are essential even in the most rigorous scientific work" (Barnard, 1936/1968, p. 306). Chess masters also are an excellent example of this point. A master or a grandmaster, when shown a chess position from a mid-game situation in a reasonable game, after looking for only five or ten seconds, usually can recognize the relationship between the pieces and propose a strong move—usually the move that objectively is best in the position (Simon, 1983).

"In any field of expertise, possession of an elaborate discrimination net that permits recognition of any one of tens of thousands of different objects or situations is one of the basic tools of the expert and the principal sources of his intuitions" (Simon, 1983, p. 26). Michael Polanyi, who coined the phrase "tacit knowing," gives the example of recognizing faces. If we know a person's face, we can recognize it among millions. Also, we can recognize the moods of the human face without being able to tell, "except quite vaguely," by what signs we know them (Polanyi, 1958). And, if we know a lot about the friend, we can make good judgments about him. Should we lend him money or not? Will we get it back if we do? Should we tell him confidential information or not? Will he keep the information to himself? If we know the friend well, we can say "yes" or "no" intuitively (Simon, 1983)?

Now, in any field in which we have gained experience, we have obtained many "friends"—patterns of different kinds of relationships that we can recognize immediately (Simon, 1983). In this process, which is vital to the acquisition of a skill, the recognition of patterns and the feelings of which we are initially aware become internalized in our tacit knowing, which cannot be specified in detail. And since *it cannot be specified in detail, it can-*

not be transmitted by procedure, since no prescription for it exists. It can be passed on only by case example (Polanyi, 1958).

A psychotherapist describes this process as follows: "Suppose I am trying to decide whether to recommend psychotherapy to a patient. In the specific instance, diagnosis is not always a good indicator of what will happen in psychotherapy. I match a patient who brings me some problems against memories of patients I have previously encountered. I have a hunch about whether psychotherapy will go or not." The therapist goes on to say, "This way of proceeding—deplorably sloppy as it may sound—works well enough in most cases so that I am not likely to turn to research, which classifies patients rather more grossly than my memory bank does, for answers to the question, Should I do psychotherapy with this particular patient? (Edelson, 1994, p. 63)

And when describing how he chooses to respond to a patient, the therapist says, "My patients' stories in all their particularity remind me of other particulars, other stories they have told me or events, characters, and scenes in my own life. It is these particulars, and the different kinds of relationships I seem to detect among them, that determine my responses to what my patients tell me" (pp. 65–66).

It is through such tacit knowledge that clinicians make clinical judgments, the qualitative recognition of situations on which their practical competence depends. A clinician's experience provides him or her with an elaborate discrimination net that permits *recognition of analogous situations.* When therapists go about the spontaneous, intuitive performances of the actions of a session, they show themselves to be knowledgeable in a special way. Often they cannot say what they know. When they try to describe it, they might find themselves at a loss, or they may produce faulty descriptions (Polanyi, 1958). Therapists' knowing is tacit, implicit in their patterns of actions and in their feel for the case with which they are dealing. It seems reasonable to say, therefore, that their knowing is in their action. As Polanyi says, "The medical diagnostician's skill is as much an art of doing as it is an art of knowing" (1958, p. 54).

SUMMARY

We can see that researchers, like practitioners, recognize that theories and techniques of psychotherapy may not directly translate into what therapists do in their therapeutic encounters. There is a disparity between theoretical descriptions and the reality to which they refer. Theories can be useful for organizing information, but they do not determine the practice of therapy. They can serve as a guide to clinical practice only if they can be integrated into the practical knowledge of doing therapy, but they cannot replace this knowledge (Polayni, 1958).

This is so because practitioners must consider many factors that cannot be predicted by theories of psychotherapy. Situations of practice are typified by unique and unpredictable events, whereas theories of psychotherapy describe general, lawful predictions. Although clinicians sometimes make use of theories and techniques, it is also true that they depend on tacit recognitions and clinical judgments. Theoretical knowledge does not account for the practical competence practitioners bring to the demands of real-world practice.

Proponents of the specific approach recognize the difference between knowing-in-theory and knowing-in-practice. They distinguish between *adherence*, which refers to how much therapists use techniques considered appropriate to their treatment approach, and *competence*, which refers to how skillfully or adequately they apply the techniques. Implicit in the distinction between adherence and competence is the recognition that therapists' expertise depends on their clinical abilities to deal with unpredictable factors. In the use of techniques therapists may vary in competence. These techniques could include such hard-to-specify behaviors as choosing the appropriate response to a patient's question, the appropriate depth of interpretation, the proper within-session context for interventions, and other therapeutic behaviors that occur over the course of treatment. Put another way, proponents of the specific approach recognize that manual-guided practice does not provide control of the factors affecting competent treatment delivery. It does not provide descriptions of the complex variables involved in the therapist behaviors that are needed to describe not only the type but also the manner and the quality of the behaviors.

Similarly, proponents of the nonspecific common approach also recognize that theory-based knowledge is different from the knowledge practitioners use in their day-to-day practice. For instance, some authors have reported that training therapists to recognize the importance of maintaining a positive alliance did not result in the kinds of therapist behavior that, as they predicted, would lead to a better alliance. "To make the alliance more useful in clinical practice, we must explore not only the pretherapy variables that influence each participant's potential to forge an alliance but also the specific therapist activities that address the different aspects of the alliance at different phases of therapy" (Horvath and Luborsky, 1993, p. 570). This could include such hard-to-specify therapist behaviors as choosing to focus on the therapeutic relationship and recognizing relationship patterns as well as the relevance of the therapist's responses. Thus, proponents of the common approach recognize that doing therapy well depends on the skillful ability of a therapist to form a therapeutic alliance.

Practitioners are, perhaps, the most vocal in drawing attention to the difference between knowing-in-theory and knowing-in-practice. Many practitioners maintain that they do not look to theory-based research for help in doing psychotherapy or for answers to questions that come to mind as they do psychotherapy. Psychotherapy research, they say, usually deals with how the world actually is, independently of any observer, rather than how things or events seem to a person. "Our theories inevitably shape what we can see, but at their most vital they are reciprocally altered by the observations themselves. Theory provides the framework that makes observation possible, but all theories eventually yield in the very face of the very data they generate" (Greenberg, 1994, p. 16).

Practitioners assert that knowledge derived from research is not useful because it usually offers general principles, whereas a therapist has to deal with the particulars of a case. To make interventions at a specific moment in the treatment of a particular patient, practitioners draw on their clinical knowledge. Clinical knowledge, practitioners say, is acquired by encountering certain cases and situations repeatedly. "Scientists may learn about the nature of things by finding out what they can do *to* them, but the clinician can learn of the true nature of man only in the attempt to do something *for* and *with* him . . . clinical evidence is grounded in the study of what is unique to the individual case—including the psychotherapist's involvement. Such uniqueness, however, would not stand out without the background of that other concern, . . . namely the study of what is *common* to verifiable *classes* of cases" (Erikson, 1964, p. 80; emphasis in original).

A practitioner's experience provides him or her with an elaborate discrimination net that permits recognition of common or analogous cases. Analogy involves fitting detailed data from one particular case to a familiar one. The familiar one functions as a metaphor, as an exemplar for the unfamiliar case (Kuhn, 1977). When experienced practitioners makes sense of a case they observe to be unique, they can see it as something already present in their repertoire of experiences. A new case is seen to be analogous to a case previously encountered.

It is their capacity to see unfamiliar cases as familiar ones that enable therapists to bring their experience to bear on the unique case. ". . . I have become more and more aware that it is the relationship between particulars, such as those from my life experience (including my experience with a particular patient), and not theory that leads me to my interventions. I am reminded by one scene or event of another that called up the same emotion. Or one scene or story has the same theme as another (for example, revenge, rivalry)" (Edelson, 1994, p. 66).

The ability of practitioners to respond emphathetically to their patients is related more to their narrative competence—to their skill to listen for stories and to find relational patterns—than to their theoretical knowledge (Edelson, 1994). Clinical competence cannot be taught by formulas. It can, however, be conveyed by case studies. Knowledge obtained from case studies, practitioners say, is more clinically relevant than general principles derived from rigorously controlled studies. Case studies can be useful because they "take pleasure in particulars and focus on their patterns" (Edelson, 1994, p. 84). A skillful supervisor draws out critical facts and patterns of relationships. This helps the student to see the unfamiliar, unique case as both similar to and different from the familiar case study. The case study functions, therefore, as a precedent, a metaphor, or an exemplar for the unfamiliar case.

Conclusions

Ever since Freud failed at giving medical readers the directions necessary to carry through his method of psychotherapy treatment, researchers and practitioners have recognized that theories of psychotherapy cannot account for what takes place when a therapist "does" psychotherapy. Researchers and practitioners have proposed different approaches to the limitations of theory-based knowledge and the related problem of the lack of clinical relevance. Both, however, recognize a common problem. Doing therapy involves more than applying techniques derived from theory-based knowledge. In clinical practice, another source of knowledge on which competent practitioners rely is their practical knowledge.

Despite this recognition, surprisingly little progress has been made in bridging the gap between theory and practice. Many writers have suggested that this lack of progress is due to conceptual limitations in the research methodologies and that what is missing are measures that specify what competent practitioners do during the moment-to-moment therapeutic encounter. Presumably, it has been the perceived difficulty of specifying the mode of thinking underlying therapists' practical competence (knowing-in-practice) that has delayed progress.

As our next task, then, we consider the modes of thought underlying knowing-in-theory and knowing-in-practice. The important question is whether there are two different forms of human thought—logical thought and analogical thought—and whether what we call knowing-in-practice relies largely on the latter.

Two Ways of Thinking

As early as 1936, in an essay titled "Mind in Everyday Affairs," Chester Barnard distinguished "logical processes" from "non-logical processes." By "logical processes" he meant thinking that could be expressed in words or other symbols, that is, reasoning. By "non-logical processes" he meant thinking that could be known only by a judgment, decision, or action. In ordinary experience, according to Barnard, the two classes of intellectual processes are not clearly separated but flow into each other.

Many philosophers also have noted the differences between the two types of thinking. Bergson contrasts "analysis" (the scientific attitude) and "intuition" (the immediate common-sense attitude). Many German philosophers are intrigued by the distinction. They sometimes speak of "nomothetic" (general) knowledge as opposed to "idiographic" knowledge (of the particular event).

The two types of thinking correspond to two modes of interest and attention of which the human mind is capable. The mind may classify its experiences and contemplate the general laws that emerge, or it may be concerned with the individual patterns of an experience. There is no contradiction between the two types of thinking, nor do they reside in different cerebral hemispheres competing for control over the mind. All serious thinking calls on both types of thinking—analytic thought and intuitive thought (Simon, 1983).

Today, psychologists refer to these complementary processes of thought as modes of cognitive functioning, each providing distinctive ways of ordering experience. "The two (though complementary) are irreducible to one another. Efforts to reduce one process to the other or to ignore one at the expense of the other inevitably fail to capture the rich diversity of thought. Each of the ways of knowing, moreover, has operating principles of its own and its own criteria of well-formedness. They differ radically in their procedures for verification" (Bruner, 1986, p. 11).

THE LOGICAL MODE

One mode—the logical, or rational, one—attempts to fulfill the ideal of a formal, mathematical system of description and explanation. It uses categorization or conceptualization and the operations by which categories are established and related to the other to form a system. At a gross level, the logico-scientific mode deals in general causes and makes use of procedures to assure verifiable reference and to test for empirical truth. Its language is regulated by requirements of consistency and noncontradiction. It regards language as a system of symbols that are composed into patterns that stand for things in the world. The application of the logical mode leads to good theory, tight analysis, logical proof, sound argument, and empirical discovery guided by reasoned hypothesis.

Applied to the clinical arena, the logical mode assumes that human behavior is understandable, predictable, controllable, and subject to the same empirical methods used in the study of formal systems. According to the logical orientation, there is an objectively knowable world, independent of the practitioner's values and views. To gain technical knowledge of it, the practitioner must maintain a clear boundary between himself and his object of inquiry. To exert technical control over it, he must observe it and keep his distance from it. His stance toward inquiry is that of spectator-manipulator. The logical orientation assumes that the objective facts about the world do not depend on the interpretation or even the presence of any person. Perception is simply viewed as a process by which facts about the world are registered in one's thoughts and feelings.

When these assumptions are stated explicitly, it becomes obvious that in many typical real-world situations, people, no matter how badly they want to, simply cannot apply the logical mode of thinking. There is much evidence suggesting that human behavior in certain choice situations departs widely from the requirements of the logical mode of thinking. The main reason for this departure is that human beings do not always have the facts nor the consistent structure of values nor the reasoning power required to apply the logical mode of thinking (Simon, 1983). As our next task, we examine what they do instead.

The Analogical Mode

The intuitive, or analogical, mode postulates that much of human thinking, and much of the success of human beings in arriving at correct decisions, is a result of analogical thinking. The analogical mode uses stories, metaphors, analogies, and so on as tools for description and explanation. Whereas the logical mode must eventuate in predicting something that is testably right, the analogical mode lacks such need for testability. Believability in a story or an analogy is of a different order from believability in a theory or a logical proposition.

The analogical mode is not just a different way of ordering experience. It also uses language differently. In the analogical mode, language is *not* regulated by requirements of consistency and noncontradiction. The term *then* functions differently in the logical proposition "if *x*, then *y*" and in the narrative statement "The man fought with his wife and then went to buy her a gift." In contrast to the logical mode, which is governed by requirements of scientific argument and usually chooses words trying to ensure clear and definite reference and literal sense, the analogical mode does not conform to the requirements of plain reference or of verifiable predictions.

Interpretive Meanings

Instead, in the analogical mode, language is regarded as a system of evocative symbols that may be somewhat ambiguous. When analogies and metaphors are used, the results are no longer amenable to being transformed into ordinary truth-functional propositions, as in such sentences as "The boy is depressed." This sentence can be translated into a formal or logical proposition and tested for its truth value. But, if an utterance is nonliteral, as in the sentence "The boy's heart hardens and grows cold," different meanings may arise and interpretive activity is evident. There is one property that all such utterances share that makes them different from logical propositions: they resist logical procedures for establishing what they mean. "They must, as we say, be *interpreted.* There is no way of arriving logically at their 'truth conditions.' . . . Interpretive meanings of the kinds

we are considering are metaphoric, allusive, very sensitive to the context"
(Bruner, 1990, pp. 60–61).

Perceiving Similar Relations

It has been recognized for some time now that analogies and metaphors
are not just a phenomenon of language but pervade all aspects of cognition.
Analogical thinking leads to connections between two events. That is to
say, it leads to seeing similarities that one did not see before so that one
can come to see relationships previously not known to exist. The dictionary
tells us that an analogy is "a relation of likeness between two things . . .
consisting in the resemblance not of the things themselves but of two or
more attributes, circumstances, or effects . . . its specific meaning is a *similarity of relations*." What matters, then, is that a relational structure can
be carried over from a familiar event to an unfamiliar event. The familiar
again functions as a metaphor, as an exemplar for the unfamiliar.

The realization that an unfamiliar event is similar to another more familiar event can enable a thinker to reach a better understanding of the
unfamiliar event by transporting knowledge from the familiar event. A scientific problem can be illuminated by the discovery of a profound analogy.
A mundane problem similarly can be solved by the retrieval of the solution
to an analogous problem. An analogy also can serve a helpful role in expo-
sition: a speaker attempting to explain a difficult notion or to describe
what someone is like can appeal to the listener's existing knowledge by
using an analogy.

Analogical reasoning can be used anywhere in the continuum from literal similarity to nonliteral similarity. If you hear somebody say, "Beth is
a block of ice," or "Jeff is a dictator," you are likely to assume that the
speaker does not mean what he says literally but that he is speaking metaphorically. Also, you are not likely to have very much trouble figuring out
what he means. Similarly, in motivation theory hydraulic models have been
used to describe levels of motivation. Water flowing out of the container
represents the level of motivation. A high motivation is analogous to high
flow rate (Toates, 1986). Obviously, a person's motivation does not consist
of pipes carrying fluids, but the relations exhibited by such an analogy
may enable conclusions to be drawn about motivational systems when the
appropriate interpretations are made. In such cases the similarity of relations between entities that intrinsically are widely different may be called

isomorphism. The isomorphism is a consequence of the fact that, in certain respects, *similar relations* can be applied to different phenomena.

The perception of similarity is not something static and well defined but something that changes with development and with the acquisition of expertise (Piaget, 1972). The results of several expert/novice studies show, for instance, that experts categorize problems differently from novices. Because of such differences, "experts are able to see the underlying similarities in a great number of problems, whereas novices see a variety of problems that they consider to be dissimilar because the surface features are different" (Chi, Feltovich, and Glaser, 1981, p. 130). In chess research, for example, it appears that experts' superiority in seeing the right move cannot be attributed to the masters' generally superior memory, for "the masters appear to be constrained by the same short-term memory as everyone else" (Chase and Simon, 1973, p. 56). Instead, their superior performance appears to lie in their ability to perceive meaningful relational patterns between the chess pieces and to encode them in a single relational structure (Chase and Simon, 1973).

The analogical mode assumes that the perception of relational patterns is the result of mental construction. The ability to identify similarity in relational structure arises because one can bring experiences to bear on a unique situation. Meaning is constructed rather than merely "read off." Put another way, it assumes that knowledge of reality, whether it is occasioned by perception, language, memory, or anything else, is a result of going beyond the information given. It arises through the *interaction* of that information within its present context with the decision maker's preexisting knowledge.

Interpretable, Unpredictable, and Autonomous

In contrast to the logical mode, which emphasizes the belief that human behavior is understandable, predictable, and controllable, the analogical mode assumes human behavior is interpretable, unpredictable, and autonomous. The analogical mode assumes individuals constantly are involved in interactions with others. Also, it assumes that prediction of a person's interactions is possible only under the most restrictive conditions. It is always possible, in principle, for a person to avoid being predicted in any interaction. Our interactions with other people and with the world we inhabit put us into situations of what Heidegger calls *throwness,* for which the image of a conversation (or meeting) is more apt than the image of the objective, detached scientist who makes observations, forms hypotheses, and consciously chooses a predictable course of action (Winograd and Flores, 1986).

Applied to the clinical arena, the analogical mode assumes that under conditions of everyday professional practice, the therapist is put in a situation of throwness bounded by the action-present. The therapist's stance toward inquiry is not that of a detached observer but that of an involved participant. Predictability and controllability, the norms of the rational mode, are achievable only in a very limited way. The therapist usually is unable to shield his or her technical actions from the effects of confounding changes in the practice situation. Changes may occur rapidly and may be beyond the control of the therapist. Variables are locked into one another so that the therapist cannot separate or predict the variables. The practice situation often is uncertain, and the very act of intervening may produce unexpected results.

In contrast to the rationalistic orientation, the analogical orientation assumes that facts are matters not of objective knowledge but of "disciplined subjectivity" (Erikson, 1964). Meaning is created by an active listening in which utterances trigger interpretations. This subjective quality derives from the therapeutic process itself, in which the patient tells the therapist stories about his or her life, and therapists' interventions are responses to how they interpret (infer) a patient's stories. The therapist's interpretations (inferences) are then tested for their plausibility and for their utility in intervention. The plausibility of an interpretation is what matters, not whether a fact is verifiable.

Summing Up

There are at least two kinds of knowledge: *knowing-in-theory* and *knowing-in-practice*. Although clinicians sometimes make use of theories, it also is true that in much of the spontaneous behavior of practice they depend on their clinical judgment to deal with the unpredictable, unique events that occur in everyday professional practice. To the extent that the spontaneity of clinicians' actions is considered crucial, theory-based knowledge apparently does not describe or account for the clinical expertise that clinicians sometimes reveal in what they do. When practitioners go about the spontaneous, intuitive performances of the practice of therapy, they show themselves to be knowledgeable in a special way. Often they cannot say

what it is that they know. When they try to describe it they may find themselves at a loss, or they may produce descriptions that are inexact. Their
knowing is tacit; it is implicit in their patterns of actions and in their feel
for the stuff with which they are dealing. It seems right to say, therefore,
that their knowing is in their practice.

This distinction between knowing-in-theory and knowing-in-practice is
recognized by both researchers and clinicians. Researchers of the unique
specific approach, for instance, acknowledge that efforts to specify treatments via manuals do not reflect all that occurs within treatment. They
admit that although much attention is paid to the careful definition of
treatment interventions, one additional aspect that needs to be included is
a measure of how *competent* a therapist is in carrying out the treatment.
Competence refers to aspects of the delivery of treatment that depend on
clinicians' clinical judgment. Implicit in the construct of competence is the
recognition that practitioners exhibit a kind of knowing-in-practice that is
unlike the kind of knowledge described in manuals and cannot be measured by the extent to which therapists *adhere* to the manual guidelines.

Also, researchers of the common nonspecific approach recognize that
theory-based knowledge is different from the knowledge practitioners use
in practice. As mentioned before, proponents of the common approach
claim there are factors common to all forms of therapy. For example, the
therapeutic alliance is thought to be a common relationship factor that cuts
across all forms of therapy. At the core of the construct of the alliance is
the notion of collaboration. The idea focuses on the importance of the
patient's and therapist's forming a partnership against the common enemy
of the client's debilitating psychological problems. This collaborative relationship is thought to foster a process conducive to patient change. Central
to the development of a good relationship is the *technical skillfulness* of a
therapist. Implicit in the construct of the therapeutic alliance, therefore,
is the recognition that a technically skillful therapist does things to maximize a collaborative relationship with a patient. Little is known, however,
about the transactions that enhance the buildup of a collaborative relationship. Thus, unfortunately, the value of this corpus of work is limited by the
failure of measures used to identify specific therapist and client behaviors
linked to a good collaborative relationship.

Practitioners also recognize that knowing-in-theory is different from
knowing-in-practice. They maintain that knowledge derived from theory is
not useful because it offers only general principles whereas they must deal

with the specific, unique events of practice. Practitioners say that the main source of knowledge on which they must rely is their clinical know-how. According to practitioners, the ability to listen to patients' stories and to find patterns is related more to clinical competence than to theoretical cognizance. Clinical competence is acquired by encountering certain situations repeatedly. This allows the practitioner to develop the ability to recognize relational patterns that describe these situations. These patterns guide therapists in what to attend to and how to respond. The capacity to recognize relational patterns enables practitioners to see unfamiliar situations as familiar ones and by that to bring their experiences to bear on the unique case.

Despite the awareness that doing psychotherapy involves more than applying theoretically based knowledge, little progress has been made in specifying what competent practitioners *do* to influence patient changes. Evidently, the chief cause for this delayed progress is the difficulty of defining the way of thinking that underlies therapists' knowing-in-practice. Although in daily practice therapists make constant use of their clinical expertise, the thinking processes behind their clinical knowledge (knowing-in-practice) remain difficult to explain. To advance our understanding of the kind of knowing in which competent practitioners engage, we examined the modes of thought underlying knowing-in-theory and knowing-in-practice.

The logical mode of thought, which underlies knowing-in-theory, attempts to fulfill the ideal of a formal system of description and explanation. Its language is regulated by consistency and noncontradiction and can be tested for its truth value. The application of the logical mode of thought leads to good theory and tight analysis. The logical mode of thought has proven its effectiveness most clearly in the hard sciences—those that explain the operation of deterministic mechanisms whose principles can be captured in formal systems.

The logical orientation supposes there is an objectively knowable world that is understandable, predictable, and controllable. A main feature of the logical orientation is the notion of objective detachment. The scientist is depicted as a detached observer who, for instance, studies the motion of planets, observes regularities, abstracts a law to represent the regularities, and devises a formal model to predict the future motion of the planets. The motion of the planets does not change as a function of the scientist's observations.

Applied to the clinical arena, the logical mode presumes that the practitioner, like the scientist, can study the patient's situation, listen to the facts, abstract the problem to be solved, and use a set of techniques to get predictable chosen ends predetermined to change the patient's situation. It assumes that the practitioner can have complete knowledge and anticipation of the consequences that will follow each technical move. Further, it assumes that to gain technical control the practitioner can maintain a stance of objective detachment.

In distinction to the logical mode, the analogical mode, which underlies knowing-in-practice, assumes that the therapist is put into a situation of *throwness* for which the image of an involved participant is more fitting than the image of a detached scientist. Through the therapist's transactions with the situation the therapist functions more as an active participant. This is another way of saying the situation the therapist seeks to understand is partly of his own making: he is *in* the situation that he seeks to understand.

According to the analogical orientation, objective knowledge, then, is an ideal that the therapist may strive for but in practice only roughly approximates. The therapist's behavior falls short of objective rationality because, in actuality, the therapist cannot predict or control the effects of actions. Indeed, this is why the rational model of decision making and the treatment manuals that we described earlier are limited for helping therapists manage the practice situation. The practice situation, having a life of its own, is distinct from the therapist's intentions and may foil the therapist's technical moves and reveal new meanings.

The analogical mode is not only a different way of being in a situation, it is also a different way of using language. In the analogical mode, language is regarded as a system of evocative symbols. Stories, metaphors, and analogies are used, and their meanings must be interpreted.

Analogies and metaphors are not just a facet of language but pervade all aspects of cognition. Perceiving similarities is central to human thought. It is crucial for recognition, categorization, and learning. The ability to perceive similarities arises because one can see the unfamiliar situation (case, object, story, thing, person, theory, idea, system, problem, event, and so on) as analogous to a familiar situation.

The realization that an unfamiliar situation is similar to another more familiar situation can enable a person to reach a better understanding of the unfamiliar situation by transporting knowledge from the familiar situation. In a reasoning mode of this kind, learning is not accomplished by merely adding new facts and making predictions about them. Rather, learning depends on the ability to identify relevant similarities that already exist.

In any field of expertise the perception of similarity is essential. As mentioned before, perceiving similarities is a basic tool of the expert. Using analogical reasoning, the psychotherapist can notice, for instance, a thematic similarity between the patient's story about the past, what is going on currently in the patient's life, and the story that the patient may be enacting in the psychotherapy situation. Also, the therapist can notice that one case is like another case he has already encountered.

What still is lacking, however, is a systematic understanding of what a psychotherapist *sees* when he identifies a similarity. The question that we need to ask is: When two situations (cases, stories, events, and so on) are perceived as similar (that are initially very different from each other), what accounts for the similarity? That is to say, we still do not know what the therapist sees when he learns to see one case as he does a case he already has encountered or when he learns to see common themes in the stories patients tell. The basis of similarity continues to be a puzzle.

As Erikson puts it, "Clinical evidence is grounded in the study of what is *unique* to the *individual* case—including the psychotherapist's involvement. Such uniqueness, however, would not stand out without the background of that other concern, which I have neglected here, namely the study of what is *common* [similar] to verifiable *classes* of cases" (Erikson, 1964, p. 80; emphasis in original).

3
Assessing Similarities

It must have required many ages to discover that a brace of pheasants and a couple of days were both instances of the number 2: the degree of abstraction involved is far from easy.

Bertrand Russell

In chapter 1, we said that research-based knowledge is useful for many goals, but its drawback is its failure to reflect what happens in practice. In chapter 2, we described the differences between these two types of knowledge, knowing-in-theory and knowing-in-practice. In clinical practice the perception of similarity is essential. Using analogical reasoning the psychotherapist sees, for example, a thematic similarity between the patient's story about the past and what is going on currently in the patient's life, or the psychotherapist sees that one case (or situation) is like another case he already has encountered, or he sees what is common to classes of cases. Psychotherapy still lacks a systematic treatment of how similarity is determined, however. What accounts for the perception of similarity between situations that on the surface may be very different?

Our aim in this chapter is to examine similarity perceptions. For our purposes, we shall denote by the term *perception* the *constructive process of assessing* the environment, of getting to know the environment. So we can use the term *assessing* interchangeably with *perceiving*.

First, we distinguish between two types of similarity perceptions—attributional similarity and relational similarity. This distinction essentially focuses on the fact that one can perceive two things (or two objects, or two people) as similar in terms of simple, superficial *attributes* (either descriptive attributes or mental attributes) or by viewing them as similar along deep, *relational* structures.

After our discussion of how similarities in general are perceived, which is needed before one can understand how it applies to the therapeutic situation, we examine how therapists map relational similarities. In later chapters we present a systematic method that can be used to operationalize patients' and therapists' assessments of attributes and relations. This method invites a new understanding of the thinking processes underlying knowing-in-practice, which in turn we hope will advance the science of psychotherapy.

Now, let us discuss the two types of similarities.

Two Types of Similarities
ATTRIBUTIONAL SIMILARITIES

When interacting with the physical and social environment, we name the objects and people in our world (dog, man, ball, and so on). And we describe these objects and people in terms of their traits or attributes (large, strong, spherical, and so on). In this way, for instance, we can classify a cocker spaniel as a medium-sized dog with large, long, fluffy ears.

The basis of similarity between objects or people may lie, therefore, in shared attributes of some kind, as in referring to different dogs (cocker spaniels and beagles) as medium-sized dogs, referring to different objects (a ball, a planet, an atom) as spherical objects, or referring to different people (a man, a woman, a boy) as strong people.

Descriptive attributes tell us something about the way objects or people may behave. A spherical object can be rolled around; if I put it on the table it might roll off. A strong person can lift heavy things; if I ask the person to lift a shovel he or she can. The descriptive attributes that we perceive are relatively invariant features and show consistent relations with other events.

The shape of a solid object or the physical strength of a person is a relatively enduring property. It is something one can depend on finding again. It is connected with lasting possibilities of the object or the person. "It allows us to predict to a certain degree how the object will behave when we handle it; for instance, if I see an object is spherical, I predict it can be rolled. This prediction is possible because shape is connected in an invariant way with a possible event, namely all spherical solid objects can be rolled" (Heider, 1958, p. 30). Similarly, if I know a person is physically strong, I predict the person can carry heavy objects.

Summarizing, we can say that descriptive attributes are helpful for naming the objects and persons in our world and for describing these objects and persons in terms of their attributes. Also, descriptive attributes are helpful for categorizing information about objects and persons. For instance, if you know a person owns an expensive house, has five cars, and buys jewelry you can assume from these facts that the person is "rich." So descriptive attributes help us characterize persons according to certain attributes (wealth, age, intelligence, weight, and so forth), which, in turn, helps us categorize information.

Finally, descriptive attributes are helpful for understanding the causal possibilities of objects and persons. Using the logical mode of thought we can predict (to a certain degree) how an object or a person will behave (for instance, a rich person is likely to spend money on luxury items or buy a house in an expensive neighborhood). If we can characterize a situation by identifiable objects or persons with well-defined descriptive properties, then we can find general rules that apply to situations in terms of those descriptive properties and make predictions about the behavior of the object or person in the situation of concern. Since descriptive attributes are connected in lawful ways with other features, predictions about behavior of the object or person become possible.

Limits of Descriptive Attributes

Descriptive attributes, however, are insufficient for making objects (including art, music, and literature) or human behavior fully intelligible. If we use only descriptive characteristics we are unable to make sense of an object's movement or a person's intentions or actions. This is so because descriptive attributes define static characteristics ("The ball is spherical" or "The woman is rich") rather than dynamic qualities.

Describing a person as rich, for instance, does not necessarily explain why the person gives money to liberal causes. Similarly, as Gardner points out, if you only glanced at an acknowledged masterpiece, speed read a story, or played but the opening bars of a musical piece, you would be thought to have missed much of value. Certain responses seem inadequate: for example, "Oh, that's a picture of a young smiling woman" for the *Mona Lisa*, "It's about a whale-hunt" for *Moby-Dick*, "I heard some birds singing" for Beethoven's *Pastoral* Symphony.

These three kinds of responses are directed at the most superficial and descriptive aspects of the work. One looks with less disfavor on comments bringing out the mysterious aspects of the lady's expression, the allegorical quality of Ahab's wish to find himself, or the use of instrumentation for emotional effects. These comments show that if we want to interpret the intention behind these works, something other than descriptive attributes is needed.

Another example to show the limits of descriptive attributes is given by Hebb's (1946) analysis of the attempts of scientists to be "objective" by attending only to the physical or space-time descriptions of animal behavior: "A thoroughgoing attempt to avoid anthropomorphic description in the study of temperament was made over a two-year [period] at the Yerkes Laboratories. A formal experiment was set up to provide records of the actual behavior of the adult chimpanzees, and from these records to get an object statement of the differences from animal to animal. All that resulted was an almost endless series of specific acts in which no order or meaning could be found" (p. 88).

When, however, the chimpanzees assumed personal characteristics so that their behaviors were perceived in terms of *emotions* and *attitudes,* meaning was brought into the array of behaviors observed: "On the other hand, by the use of frankly anthropomorphic concepts of emotion and attitude one could quickly and easily describe the peculiarities of the individual animals. . . . Whatever the anthropomorphic terminology may seem to imply about conscious states in the chimpanzee, it provides an intelligible and practical guide to behavior. The objective categorization therefore missed something in the behavior of the chimpanzee that the ill-defined categories of emotion and the like did not—some order, or relationship between isolated acts that is essential to comprehension of the behavior. . . . A discussion of jealousy in the earthworm is obvious nonsense, but not in primates" (p. 88).

Mental Attributes

These examples show that if we want to interpret the meaning of behavior other types of attributional properties are needed to describe them. These other types of attributional properties are called *psychological,* or *mental, attributes* such as personality traits (dispositions), motives, attitudes, emotions, wishes, and sentiments. Mental attributes define dynamic qualities, whereas descriptive attributes define static properties. The interpretation of behavior in terms of mental attributes, as Hebb showed, often enhances understanding of that behavior.

As a dispositional property, a mental attribute enables one to grasp an unlimited variety of behavioral manifestations ("sociable," "jealous," and so on) by a single attribute (Heider, 1958; Mischel, 1990). Also, a mental attribute is assumed to show a modest degree of intrinsic invariance. For instance, the impression that a person is sociable (or a monkey is jealous), which may be conveyed in any number of ways, points to a relatively enduring characteristic of the person.

Also, insofar as mental attributes are connected in lawful ways with other features, predictions about behavior of the person become possible. Just as one can predict the rolling behavior of the ball because its spherical shape is a persisting property, so one can predict (albeit with less confidence) that a sociable person will enjoy being in the company of others because of his sociable nature, which is an enduring personality trait (or a jealous monkey will act possessively because of his jealous nature) (Heider, 1958). In their simplest form, mental attributes and their behavioral expressions are assumed by definition to correspond directly: the more a person has a sociable (or jealous) disposition, for example, the more sociable (possessive) the behavior will be.

Summarizing, we can say that mental attributes are helpful for understanding the dynamic aspects of behavior. They bring consistency and meaning to an array of behavior. Mental attributes such as motives, personality traits, and wishes are the core processes that manifest themselves in overt behavior. The manifestations are then directly grasped by the observer in terms of these psychological core processes. They would otherwise remain indecipherable (Heider, 1958). If your arm is raised above your head there is little that may be said about your motives. Your action is merely a spatiotemporal shape. In contrast, if another person were before you crouching and grimacing, suddenly it becomes possible to speak of you as aggressive or ruthless. With the aid of mental attributes your movements may now be deciphered, which in turn brings meaning to your behavior and enhances prediction of future behaviors.

Limits of Mental Attributes

The conceptualization of behavior in terms of mental attributes is extremely useful for many goals, but its limits have been noted. Heider (1958) has most articulately argued that personality traits, motives, emotions, wishes, and sentiments are psychological entities: "They are not measured by a ruler, weighed by a scale, nor examined by a light meter" (p. 32). They are mentalistic concepts, so-called intervening variables that describe an array of behavior. We are able to measure descriptive attributes (for instance, the size or weight of a person) much more easily than we can measure mental attributes (for instance, the actual strength of a wish or motive) (Heider, 1958).

Other critics have argued that although observers may agree that a given trait exists (that is, high reliability may be achieved), they cannot say what the basis for their decision is. The particular behavioral data on which the judgments or perceptions of the other person's emotions, wishes, motives, or traits are based depend on subjective inference. The observer may be hard-pressed to point at, to communicate, the basis for a decision (Hammond, 1955).

Still others have noted the lack of simple objective methods to define mental attributes. If descriptions of behavior are used to define traits, or wishes, or motives, which in turn are offered as explanations of the same behavior from which they were inferred in the first place, the circularity of the reasoning ("The chimpanzee acts possessively because of his jealous nature. The chimpanzee is jealous because he is acting possessively") becomes embarrassing, as noted, for example, by Bandura (1969).

Besides the issue of how to define mental attributes objectively, some critics have raised the issue of whether mental attributes are really useful for prediction. Although mental attributes show some degree of invariance when compared to descriptive attributes, they are less likely to yield evidence of cross-situational consistency. If predictive precision is the goal, the particular classes of conditions have to be considered much more carefully and seem to be narrower and more local than traditional mental attribute theories assumed. Humans and animals, these critics argue, show far less cross-situational consistency in their behavior than has been assumed by mental attribute theories (Mischel, 1990).

Finally, beyond the empirical critiques questioning the objectivity and predictive utility of mental attributes is the practice of endowing mental attributes in explanations of movement in inanimate objects. It has been shown, for instance, that when observers are presented with geometrical figures that move in chaotic ways the movement remains largely unintelligible. When, however, the geometrical figures assume personal characteristics so their movements are perceived in terms of motives and sentiments, a unified structure appears.

To illustrate, let us consider a celebrated monograph written by the Belgian student of perception, Baron Michotte. By cinematic means, he demonstrated that when objects move with respect to one another, observers *see* mental attributes. By means of special technical equipment Michotte made two (or more) little colored rectangles (rectangle A and rectangle B) move along a horizontal slot. He could change the direction, extent, and speed of movement at will and thus obtain an infinite variety of kinetic combinations.

As for the results, Michotte found that subjects "did not content themselves with merely describing in an objective fashion what they saw in the apparatus, saying, for example, that they saw 'A pushing B forward' but they often had an obvious tendency to complete these indications by comparisons with human or animal actions, comparisons that implied emotional states, attitudes, tendencies attributed to the objects . . . the experiments gave rise to interpretations of this nature: 'It is as though B was afraid when A approached, and ran off', or 'A joins B, then they fall out, have a quarrel, and B goes off by himself'" (Michotte, 1950, p. 115).

Similar experiments by Heider and Simmel (1944) confirmed that this kind of behavior frequently occurs. Observers spontaneously project mental attributes onto inanimate phenomena. Why this tendency to translate inanimate phenomena into mentalistic terms?

One possible explanation may be that in these cases the observers are faced with a scene or an event in which two objects (or two people, or one person and one thing) take part, each *moved in relation* to the other. Observers are faced with seeing relations between objects, and their reactions are *judgments about those relations*. When we see a relation between two objects we "read" it in terms of mentalistic attributes. This is evident in statements such as "It is as though B was afraid when A approached" or "A joins B, then they fall out, have a quarrel, and B goes off by himself."

The mental attributes ("B was afraid"; "They fall out") that observers project onto the objects are judgments about the relation "distance." We are afraid, sometimes, when an object or a person approaches us. We move away from an object or from a person we do not like or with whom we are quarreling. Thus, we can say that the reactions of the observers that are expressed in mentalistic terms are mainly relational interpretations (for example, "B is afraid to get close to A" or "When A and B quarrel, B moves away"). Such statements show that the observers are assessing the relation distance.

This is only one example of a relational interpretation. We have many ways of expressing relational assessments, especially in human relations. For instance, we might say someone is aloof, or cold, or indifferent, or detached, or withdrawn, or unapproachable. Or we might say someone has a wish "to be distant from others," "to be his own person," "to be left alone," or "to not express himself" (Luborsky and Crits-Christoph, 1990). If we examine these mentalistic terms, we find they are all ways of assessing the relation distance.

Although we speak in mentalistic terms, we do not "see" wishes, intentions, and motives; we see relations. Mentalistic attributes, which purport to describe individual traits, are not strictly applicable to the individual but rather describe relations between individuals (or objects). However, because we are focusing on the movement of just one object or one person rather than the relation itself, we speak of that person (or object) as having wishes, intentions, and motives, as if these are static properties of individual selves. In effect, what we label as mental attributes are primarily assessments of relations.

RELATIONAL SIMILARITIES

It seems appropriate at this juncture to examine *relations* more closely. As mentioned earlier, when interacting with the physical and social environment, we name the objects in our world (dog, man, table) and we describe these objects in terms of their attributes (large, strong, spherical). But this is not all we do. We assess our relationship to the things and the people around us, too.

To illustrate, suppose you are walking down the street late at night and see a stray dog. Besides categorizing the dog according to certain descriptive or mental attributes (for example, "It is a large, vicious dog") it is likely you would also assess the behavior of the dog in relation to yourself: "Is this large, vicious dog behaving in a friendly or aggressive manner toward me?" Put another way, when we interact with our social environment, we want to predict what will occur and to plan our thoughts and actions; therefore, we assess relations.

So while making sense of our world, we classify behavior into relations, for example, closeness ("She is very intrusive"); distance ("She likes to be alone"); dominance ("He orders me around"); and mutuality ("She is very cooperative"). People use language to express these relations. The statement "You are a bossy person" expresses the relation "dominance." We use these relations to describe behavior between people and between ourselves and others and to assess what a behavior means (Bassili, 1976; Giacomo and Weissmark, 1986, 1987; Katsenelinboigen, 1984).

For instance, the following behaviors occur between a woman and her friend. She discovers that her friend has gone into her briefcase, was snooping around her desk, and secretly called her co-workers. She assesses these behaviors to mean her friend is "intrusive" and is overstepping the boundaries of their relationship (is too close). Relations also are assessed through mental representations of what might happen. For example, a woman may think her friend may be going into her briefcase or eavesdropping on her phone conversations, and just the thought of these things occurring triggers her to assess the relation as intrusive.

A person's relational assessments are useful for systematizing a variety of experiences. For instance, a woman may assess as intrusion her child's entering her room without knocking, her husband's reading her mail, or her supervisor's asking about her intimate life. The woman assesses the relation as intrusion although the occasions are different and the particular behaviors are different. This is so because perceptions of relations are isomorphic. That is to say, we can apply *similar relations to different behaviors and phenomena.*

Whether in one's personal life or in psychotherapy the assessment of relational similarities among different phenomena provides us with a way to perceive and experience much of the world. This applies equally to persons who happen to be psychotherapists. Returning now to the question we posed earlier, "What accounts for the perception of similarity between situations that on the surface may be very different?" we may now venture a more specific answer: "The therapist perceives relational similarities in a person's assessments."

Different schools of psychotherapy use various terms such as *thematic affinity, common theme, core conflict, core-organizing principle, stable belief, maladaptive assumption, nuclear script, prototype, schema,* and *unity-thema* to describe the patterns in a person's relational assessments. A thematic affinity, for example, is described (to paraphrase one author) as follows:

> A patient arrives late to a psychotherapy session, then tells a story about her current difficulties in completing a work assignment on time. The story about the work assignment serves the purpose of countering the disapproval the patient imagines the psychotherapist feels in response to her coming late. The psychotherapist is reminded of stories the patient has told in other sessions illustrating how her father dominated and criticized her and how she devised secret strategies for defeating him. Thus, the psychotherapist notices a thematic

affinity between these stories about the past, what is going on currently in her work life, and the situation the patient seems to be enacting in the psychotherapy situation. (Edelson, 1994, p. 76)

These statements tell us the psychotherapist notices a similarity in the
patient's stories that he terms a "thematic similarity." He notices an invariance that underlies her manifest actions. But it is impossible to know what
remains invariant, what is similar. The concept "thematic similarity" lacks
specificity. To be specific we have to look at the patient's relational assessments. Note that the psychotherapist notices that the patient assesses the
relation "dominance." He observes that the patient assesses as dominant
her father's criticisms, her required work assignments, and her therapist's
disapproval. We may thus say the patient's assessment of the relation dominance is the invariance discovered by the therapist that he calls a thematic
similarity.

One other illustration may be helpful here. A maladaptive assumption
is described as follows:

Maladaptive assumptions underlie patients' automatic thoughts. To
identify these maladaptive assumptions, the therapist can listen
closely for themes that seem to cut across several different situations
or problem areas. Such assumptions are usually "if-then" premises
that can be inferred from patterns of automatic thoughts and behavioral responses that occur across various situations. To illustrate how
these assumptions are inferred from themes found in negative automatic thoughts, consider a depressed person who reported sadness
and being mad at herself for depending on her spouse so much. She
reported thinking, "I am mad at myself for being in this position all
the time. Like I want to leave him or . . . not depend so much on
him." She also reported that she felt manipulated by the therapist.
". . . I felt like I was changed from one mood so easily to another. . . .
I felt like I could be manipulated and that was like—I don't know.
I don't want to be easily led." The therapist provided a summary of
the two key themes he had identified from listening to the patient's
automatic thoughts about her husband and about therapy. The first
theme was fear of being controlled by other people. (Young, Beck,
and Weinberger, 1993, p. 259)

These statements tell us the psychotherapist identifies a maladaptive assumption underlying the patient's thoughts. Because the term *maladaptive
assumption* lacks specificity, the therapist uses the term *theme* to explain

the invariance that cuts across the patient's thought. But as we noted in our previous example, *theme* lacks specificity, too. In this instance, though, the therapist provides us with a theme based on the inference that the patient fears "being controlled by other people." But the problem with this statement is that another therapist may have said the patient "wishes to be independent," and another therapist may have said the patient "wishes not to be bossed around by others." Are these two (themes) statements the same, similar, or different? (Luborsky and Crits-Christoph, 1990)

Specifying the patient's relational assessment avoids such ambiguities by applying relations (for example, dominance) to different behaviors so that comparison between different statements is possible. Knowing that the patient assesses the relation "dominance" tells us that these statements all tap the same relation.

Whether it is termed a thematic similarity, a maladaptive assumption, or a person-schema, the point is the therapist identifies an underlying similarity in relational structure. That is to say, similarity in relational structure can be found between patients' stories without any known similarity in descriptive or mental attributes. The particular characters, behavior, or facts involved may be different, yet the therapist can identify a structural similarity between story A and story B. Take the previous example, where story A is "I am mad at myself for being in this position all the time," followed by story B, "I felt like I was changed [by the therapist] from one mood so easily. . . . I felt like I could be manipulated."

Though the descriptive information in the stories is obviously different, the therapist sees a similarity in relational structure. Through analogical reasoning the therapist understands one kind of story in terms of another; he interprets the meaning of them. It is not that story A is a subset of story B. Feeling manipulated by a therapist and feeling dependent on a husband are different kinds of things—and the behaviors performed are different kinds of actions. But story A is partially structured, understood, performed, and talked about in terms of the relation "dominance." These descriptions, these stories people tell about troublesome situations implicitly carry relations with them (that the therapist perceives as similar).

When the therapist makes sense of the stories, he maps the relevant relational structure from one story to the other. As in the cases we considered, the language in which the story is told may offer clues to the relation that set the problem of the story. But the surface language of the story need not contain the word *dominance,* though dominance is the relevant relation that underlines the story. The relevant relation, in this sense, is the relation that accounts for centrally important features of the story—that makes it understandable that certain elements of the situation are included in the story while others are omitted.

The claim that people perceive relational similarities also can be seen through metaphors, proverbs, and myths. Every culture has stories and metaphors that make use of relations. Perhaps an example from a classic metaphor will help convey the importance of perceiving relational similarities.

Consider the well-known example cited by Sticht: "'The Lord is my shepherd. . . .' In this case, we can imagine that the psalmist who is trying to convey his feelings about the Lord faces crowds who are familiar with the ways of shepherds. They know that shepherds take care of sheep, they protect them, take them to good pastures, and so forth. The psalmist wonders how he can convey something about the Lord to his audience. So he thinks, 'Well, the Lord takes care of me like a shepherd takes care of sheep.' Without hesitation, then, the psalmist tells the audience: 'The Lord is my shepherd . . .' and so on. In this case, he intends the audience to recognize that the Lord is someone who will take care of them, protect them, love them, and so forth" (Sticht, 1979, p. 477). The relevant relation that makes this metaphor understandable is the relation "dominance."

It is generally assumed that the context of the statements and the situation will guide the audience to the intended interpretation of the statement. Further, it may be at least tacitly understood by the psalmist that the use of a metaphorical relation is likely to cause the audience to interpret beyond those statements that can be literally expressed, and therefore a degree of affect may accompany the interpretation that would be lost if the psalmist simply listed the descriptive or mental attributes of the Lord (Sticht, 1979).

From all this, it follows that people can map relational similarity and assess the value of a relation (Katsenelinboigen, 1984). A dominant relation, for instance, can be assessed positively—"The Lord is my shepherd"—or it can be assessed negatively—"The Lord is dictatorial." The psalmist assumed his audience would assess being taken care of and being protected positively. But it is possible that someone might assess it negatively in the sense of being controlled by a dominant figure. The point is, any relation can be assessed either positively or negatively. A close relationship, for instance, can be assessed as intrusive versus intimate, a distant relationship as uninvolved versus private, a spontaneous relationship as impulsive versus carefree, a deliberate relationship as rigid versus planned.

To drive home this point still further, let us look at our earlier example again. Suppose the following behaviors occur between a woman and her friend. She discovers that her friend has gone into her briefcase, was snooping around her desk, and secretly called her co-workers. She interprets these behaviors to mean her friend is "intrusive" and is overstepping the boundaries of their relationship. She assesses the relation "closeness" negatively. But suppose she discovers that her friend was putting a gift in her briefcase? Her angry response may change to one of gratitude because she perceives the relationship to be intimate rather than intrusive.

For every relation (for example, close or distant; dominant or mutual) there are various positive or negative assessments (values). We saw that the relation "dominance" can be assessed, for example, negatively ("I feel manipulated by the therapist"; "I feel bad that I depend on my husband too much"; "I resent my father's criticisms") or positively ("The Lord is my shepherd"; "I feel my husband [or the Lord or my father] takes good care of me"; "I appreciate my father's critiques"). Because we can give different values to a relation, relational structures may appear to look different. The variety of values produces a variety of surface appearances.

The value we give to a relation is undoubtedly due to many factors concerning the needs of the person interacting with the social environment. The surrounding environment is not independent from the assessments we choose. There is a relation between what we assess and the context. In a society with no married couples fidelity is assessed differently. In a kibbutz family closeness is assessed differently, and so on. Thus, although the relations are universal, the values given to relations vary with the context and culture. Also, we should mention that a person is not necessarily aware or articulate about the assessments he or she places on a relation.

In closing, we have tried to show that assessing relations is an essential human activity. It is vital for planning our thoughts and actions and for managing and structuring phenomena. When interacting with our social environment we use trait and mental attributes to describe the things and the people around us, and we use relations to assess our relationships to the things and the people around us. The relations we use are bipolar—close versus distant, dominance versus mutuality, and so on. These contrasting poles tell us what is being distinguished.

We also have tried to show that each relation can be construed either positively or negatively. People place values on the ends of their poles. For instance, the pole "distance" can be assessed positively as "needing my private space" or negatively as "uninvolved in the relationship." Joan feels it is important to have her space and therefore views distance positively, whereas her friend Jeff feels it means that Joan is uninvolved in their relationship and therefore views distance negatively. So long as every act of assessment involves giving a value to a relation, it involves a self-determined choice. Because assessments are partly self-determined, people can effect changes in themselves and their situations through their own efforts (Bandura, 1977). As we explore relational assessments further in the next chapter we will examine the dynamics of this process. How do our assessments evolve?

Summing Up

The essence of analogical thinking is perceiving likeness. The basis of likeness may lie in shared *attributional similarities*. One type of attributional similarity is *descriptive attributes* of objects or persons (size, shape, weight, occupation, and so on).

Descriptive attributes are of use to us because they allow us to make mappings about what properties the objects or the persons will have. If we can characterize objects or persons with well-defined descriptive attributes, then by using the logical mode of thought, we can predict how they will behave. This prediction is possible because the descriptive attributes that we perceive are relatively invariant features, and they show constant relations with other events.

But descriptive attributes are less useful for understanding the meaning of behavior. As Hebb (1946) proposed, scientists attempting to account for animal behavior should not be concerned with an animal's actual bodily movements (their *descriptive properties*). The study of animal movements, according to Hebb, would be an absurdity; we should scarcely be able to understand behavior if it were described in terms of its velocity, direction, and the like. Rather, scientists should furnish accounts of what animals are attempting, trying, intending, or thinking (their *mental attributes*).

Mental attributes are of use to us because they allow us to characterize the dynamic aspects of a person's behavior across seemingly diverse situations. For instance, the impression that a person is sociable, which may be conveyed in any number of ways, points to an enduring characteristic. Just as one can predict the rolling behavior of a ball because its spherical shape is an enduring descriptive attribute, so one can predict (albeit with less confidence) that a person will be friendly because of his sociable nature, an enduring mental attribute (Heider, 1958).

But over the last two decades the mentalistic approach to behavior has been challenged for lacking objectivity, for the circularity of the reasoning, for the limited utility of inferring broad context-free mental attributes from behavioral signs as the basis for trying to predict a person's specific behavior, and for the practice of projecting mental attributes onto inanimate phenomena. To illustrate this last issue, we discussed the work of Baron Michotte. We concluded that *mental explanations are mainly assessments (interpretations) of relations.*

We noted that relations are of use to us because they allow us to describe behavior between people and between ourselves and others. We discussed how relations are useful for ordering a variety of experiences or behaviors. The same relation, we suggested, can be applied to different behaviors.

We pointed out that assessing relational similarities applies also to persons who happen to be psychotherapists. We gave two examples to show how therapists detect relational similarities in patients' stories. Though the descriptive information in the patients' stories was different, the therapist identified an underlying relational similarity. We showed through these examples that people also assess the value of a relation. The same relation can arouse different assessments. A dominant relation, for example, can be assessed positively ("The Lord will take care of me") or negatively ("The Lord is domineering").

Each person assesses a relation according to his or her individual style, his or her way of "being in the world." The positive or negative valuations attached to relations, our assessments of them, enormously influence our behavior. The values a person gives to a relation define for him what he says and does.

Assessing relations is a dynamic process involving development and change. As we explore the assessment of relations further in the next chapter we will examine the dynamics of this process.

4
Assessment Styles

It is the action of an uneducated person to reproach others for his own misfortunes; of one starting his education to reproach himself; and of one completely educated, to reproach neither others nor himself.

Epictetus

In chapter 1, we described the gap between theory-based descriptions of psychotherapy and the practice of psychotherapy. In chapter 2, we noted that a key feature of analogical thought is the ability to perceive similarity. A therapist can see, for example, a thematic similarity between a patient's story about the past and what is going on currently in the patient's life. We noted, however, that what is still lacking in the literature is a systematic treatment of how similarity is determined. Therefore, in chapter 3, we focused on how people perceive similarities. We distinguished between two types of similarity perceptions—attributional similarity and relational similarity. We reviewed how people use relations to describe behavior and to assess what a behavior means. We showed that similar relations can be applied to different behaviors and phenomena, and we illustrated that therapists perceive similar relational assessments in peoples' stories.

In this chapter, our aim is to explore further how people assess relations. We begin by showing that relational assessments are multidimensional evaluations and that three crucial dimensions on which relations are assessed are the external-internal, the reactive-selective, and the unconditional-conditional. We then discuss how a person's relational assessments evolve over time. We also illustrate what assessing relations means in everyday interactions with other people. We then distinguish between two kinds of assessments styles, the passive-observant profile (P1)and the active-participatory profile (P2).

Assessing Relations: Three Crucial Dimensions

In chapter 3, we said that descriptive attributes were insufficient for making objects or human behavior fully intelligible and that that is so because descriptive attributes define *static* characteristics.

Relations alone, however, are insufficient for interpreting or predicting the meaning of interpersonal behaviors. In our everyday relations, we take the conditions of our relational assessments into account also. We may be concerned with the circumstances of these conditions. For instance, it makes a great deal of difference whether you think the dog is aggressive because your presence suddenly scared him or because he is looking for something to prey on; whether you believe you can alter the dog's aggressive behavior or whether you feel powerless to change the situation; whether you believe the dog is aggressive because all dogs of that breed are aggressive or because you believe the dog may have been mistreated.

The assessments of these conditions bear on your actions. If you believe, for instance, that the dog is aggressive, or that you are powerless to change the situation, or that the dog is looking for something to prey on, you would probably try to avoid the dog. On the other hand, if you believe the dog was mistreated, or you can change the dog's aggressive behavior, or the dog is afraid of strangers, you might approach the dog and perhaps try to console him.

These illustrations show that people assess the conditions of their relationships. In more precise terms, we can say that three crucial dimensions on which relationships are assessed are the conditional-unconditional, the internal-external, and the selective-reactive.

- Conditional-unconditional refers to the circumstances of a relationship. People who believe relationships depend on circumstances are conditional ("The dog is aggressive because he was mistreated"; "He can go into my briefcase only to leave me a gift"). People who believe relationships are independent of the circumstances are unconditional ("The dog is aggressive because all dogs of that breed are aggressive"; "Don't ever go into my briefcase").

- Internal-external is about assuming responsibility for a relationship. People who feel responsible for a relationship are internal ("The dog is aggressive because I frightened him"; "I left my briefcase open"). Those who do not feel responsible are external ("The dog is aggressive because he is looking for something to prey on"; "He went into my briefcase").

- Selective-reactive describes the ability to change a relationship. People who feel unable to change a relationship are reactive ("There is nothing I can do to change the dog's aggressive nature"; "No matter what I do or tell him, he goes into my briefcase"). People who believe they can change a relationship are selective ("If I pet the dog he will stop being aggressive"; "I stop him from going into my briefcase").

These three dimensions are the basic components of our relational assessments. The dimensional alternatives differ qualitatively—that is, it matters whether we assess that a dog is aggressive because of his breed (external) or because something frightened him (internal); whether we assess that a person went into our briefcase to leave us a gift (conditional) or because the person always snoops around in our things (unconditional); whether we assess the intrusive relationship as one we can change (selective) or as one we are powerless to change (reactive). Dimensional assessments have disparate implications that are likely to influence our actions, feelings, and thoughts.

THE CONNECTION AMONG ACTIONS, FEELINGS, AND THOUGHTS

Actions, feelings, and thoughts come together in the theory of assessing relations. As mentioned earlier, each person assesses the value of a relation according to his or her individual style. The same relation can elicit different assessments. For example, one person may assess a close relationship as intimate, whereas another person may assess a close relationship as intrusive. Both people are assessing the same relation (closeness); it is their assessments, the value they give the relation, that differ. One assesses closeness as *positive* ("We are intimate"), the other as *negative* ("She is intrusive"), and it is these values that are linked with a person's emotion system. A person who assesses closeness negatively may react angrily if her friend asks her about her private life; by contrast, a person who assesses closeness positively may react delightedly.

Another example that shows the link between relational assessments and emotions was mentioned before. One person may assess a dominant relation as positive ("The Lord takes care of me"), whereas another person may assess a dominant relation as negative ("The Lord is dictatorial"). When the psalmist used the metaphorical relation "The Lord is my shepherd," he assumed that his audience would assess dominance positively. That is to say, he assumed that a degree of *positive emotion* would accompany the audience's relational assessment. These examples suggest that assessing a relation is more than just a cognitive process. It includes actions, feelings, and thoughts.

The psychological process of assessing relations is not intended to be limited to that which is ordinarily called cognitive, emotional, or behavioral. Rather, assessing relations is a superordinate process representing the varied connections among actions, feelings, and thoughts, as weather is a superordinate happening for the connections among wind, velocity, humidity, temperature, barometric pressure, and form of precipitation (Kagan, 1989; Kelly, 1955).

To illustrate the connections among feelings, actions, and thoughts, imagine that your friend goes into your briefcase, snoops around your desk, and reads your mail. You might get angry and tell her to mind her business. In terms of your assessments, what you have done is to lump all three of your friend's behaviors into the relational assessment "intrusiveness." Your angry feelings reflect the negative pattern of values you give to the relation "intrusion," which in turn guides your behavioral response of telling your friend to mind her business.

Thus, your cognitive evaluation ("I don't like someone intruding into my things"); your affective response ("I am angry"); and your action ("Mind your business") all share a common currency, namely, the negative assessment of the relation "intrusive." The values a person gives to a relation define for him what he feels, says, and does.

THE TENDENCY OF RELATIONAL ASSESSMENTS TO BE AUTOMATIC

As we have just seen, an emotional response occurs when a person assesses a relation. It is in this sense that there is a cognitive basis for emotions. The claim that emotions involve cognitive assessments of relations is different from asserting that the contribution of cognition is necessarily a deliberate, conscious process.

For the most part, our relational assessments are automatic (implicit). If we were asked about our relational assessments we probably would be unable to make a list of them. There is a widespread view in social cognition that animals and people are capable of such automatic assessments, in contrast with the deliberate and conscious processes of assessing relational meaning.

LeDoux (1989) refers to these automatic assessments as "subcortical" (reaching only as far as the amygdala). Others use different terms, for example, "affordances" (Baron and Boudreau, 1987), "resonances" (Shepard, 1984), "intersubjectivities" (Trevarthen, 1979), and "embodied intelligence" (Merleau-Ponty, 1962). Heidegger's distinction between being in a situation and observing oneself as an outsider is also apt here. The distinction between automatic and deliberate modes of assessing relational value has also been described by others who have been interested with emotion theory.

The key theme of all this is that somehow, without elaborate and deliberate cognitive processing or even being conscious of doing so, we automatically assess the value of our person-environment relationships (Lazarus, 1991). *Automatic* here implies that people react with an emotion when assessing the value of their relationships (which, in turn, as noted above, influences their overt behaviors).

This point is recognized by authors of literature, which thrives on the imagined emotions and behaviors of its characters. Varying an example from Ortony, Clore, and Collins (1988), the basic scenario is simple: The author describes a relation that readers recognize as being important to a character as regards the relational assessment that the character is known or assumed to have made. The character is portrayed as assessing a relation as positive or negative. Typically the character is described as having a very strong affective reaction to a situation that challenges his or her valenced assessment. Finally, the valenced assessment with the affective reaction usually results in some sort of change in the character's judgment or behavior.

Consider, for example, the main plot of *Othello*. We start with the assumption that Desdemona's fidelity is important for Othello. The reader assumes that Othello assesses the relation "loyalty" positively. We can infer this from what Othello says. For example, his statements, "I had rather be a toad, And live upon the vapour of a dungeon, Than keep, a corner in the thing I love For others' uses . . . If she [Desdemona] be false, O, then heaven mocks itself!" Here Othello is metaphorically expressing the positive value he places on Desdemona's faithfulness.

One day Desdemona drops a handkerchief, her first gift from Othello, who had begged her to guard it closely. Emilia finds it, but Iago takes the handkerchief and places it in Casio's room. Iago then convinces Othello that Desdemona has given it to Casio, and he also convinces Othello that Casio and Desdemona are lovers. Desdemona is afraid to admit that she has lost the handkerchief and makes evasive replies when questioned by her husband.

Othello then incorrectly concludes that Desdemona is having an affair with Casio. This threatens Othello's strongly valenced assessment of "loyalty." He becomes consumed with anger and jealousy and says to Desdemona: "Come, swear it damn thyself; Lest being like one of heaven, the devils themselves Should fear to seize thee: therefore be double-damn'd; Swear thou art honest . . . Heaven truly knows that thou art false as hell." The result is a dramatic deterioration in judgment and a correspondingly drastic action in which Othello kills both Desdemona and himself.

Clearly, Shakespeare can reliably produce in readers an awareness of a character's affective state (Othello's anger and jealousy) by portraying a situation whose relational assessment (positive assessment of loyalty) is assumed to give rise to it. This suggests that writers use an implicit theory that individual emotions can be specified in terms of relational assessments that are sufficient to produce them. Thus, writers do not always have to state what emotions a character is experiencing because when the described situation contains the relational assessment for a particular emotion, the emotion can be inferred from the assessment. The fact that millions of readers, often over centuries, all infer similar emotions from the described relational assessment suggests that this implicit theory cannot be too far wrong (Ortony, Clore, and Collins, 1988).

Empirical research has produced sizable support for this implicit theory by showing strong connections between emotion, behavior, and the assessment of relations. Among the relations studied intensively is the relation "attachment" (closeness)-"separation" (distance).

Researchers studying attachment have developed simple procedures for measuring the affective nature of the attachment relation in a laboratory context. The procedure of briefly separating an infant from its mother has been a key experimental method in the study of attachment. The fact that researchers can reproduce the relation in a laboratory context suggests that relations can easily be *objectified*. It also suggests that researchers can reliably produce individuals' affective states by creating a laboratory situation whose relational assessment is assumed to produce them.

The most extensive studies of attachment have been provided by the British psychiatrist John Bowlby (and by a series of experiments by Harry Harlow). The essence of attachment, according to Bowlby, is the maintenance of proximity to the caregiver, usually the mother. This proximity can be in terms of physical contact (for example, touching the mother) or psychological contact (for example, seeing the mother and knowing that she is close by). Besides maintaining proximity, the baby performs a set of attachment *behaviors,* including babbling, smiling, looking at the care-taker, and following or clinging to him or her. One main characteristic of attachment to a person, then, is an effort to approach or maintain proximity to that person. A second characteristic is *distress*—protest and increased heart rate (suggesting emotional arousal) when the infant is separated from the individual to whom it is attached.

The full range of relations relevant to our emotional-behavioral system must be very large (certainly larger than just the relation "attachment"), yet we lack systematic enumeration and classification. Although some researchers have recognized the importance of assessing relations, we still do not have systematic classifications of the different types of relations. Most existing efforts to develop relational classification systems focus on the person and the environment separately. How one classifies person-environment relationships depends on one's analytic purposes, and most of these do not direct us toward the elementary psychological relationships that underlie our assessments.

Although there are many references in the literature to relational patterns (for instance, as mentioned before, terms like *schemas, core conflict, common theme,* and *prototype* are used to refer to patterns in a person's relational assessments), these terms do not specify the basic relationships. Also, although there are many references in the literature to contrasting types of relationships (for instance, the contrast between passive-dependent with aggressive relationships between persons; competitive, self-centered relationships with those characterized by mutuality; symbiotic with independent relationships; and rigid relational patterns with flexible ones), academic psychology has neglected to develop a systematic, operational measure of the different types of relationships.

Consequently, psychotherapy researchers have been prevented from studying how therapists help patients change their relational assessments during therapy. To advance this line of research, we developed a measure that operationalizes different types of relationships. In later chapters, we show how it can be used for measuring a person's relational assessments, and we also illustrate how it can be used to study therapeutic change. But here, we should like to explore further how a person's relational assessments change across the life span. We then examine differences in assessment styles. Specifically, we look at the differences between the passive-observant assessment style and the active-participatory assessment style.

The Development of Relational Assessments

Enough has already been said to make clear that there are various ways of assessing relations. Two persons may see the same relation (closeness), but the values they give it may differ. One may assess closeness positively ("We are intimate"), whereas the other may assess closeness negatively ("She is intrusive"). The assessments one applies to the things and the people around them evolve over time.

In general, a person's relational assessments develop as he or she interprets the replicative features of experience. To illustrate how relational assessments evolve, let us look again at the relation "closeness"-"distance." We will show how the assessment of closeness-distance changes as one grows from childhood through adolescence and into adulthood.

Babies younger than seven months rarely cry when their mothers leave them (distance). Between twelve and fifteen months, however, the experience is almost sure to bring distress and tears—and then the impact begins to weaken. Developmental psychologists refer to a baby's negative assessment of distance, that is, mother leaving, as "separation anxiety." Changes in the assessment of distance seem to appear as an outgrowth of a child's newly developed intellectual skills. These skills allow the child to successively construe and reconstrue the experiences of his or her life (Kagan and Segal, 1968). At eight months, most babies are able for the first time not only to call to mind past events but also to compare them with the here and now. When mother leaves (distance), they can now recall her former presence (closeness)—and simultaneously realize that she is no longer there (distance). Being unable to understand this discrepancy, they become anxious and cry. Later, when babies also can anticipate that mother will return, the discrepancy is more easily resolved, and their negative assessment of distance begins to fade.

As the child grows, his or her relational assessments continue to evolve. Eventually the child's assessments are those by which he or she maintains individuality. During adolescence, children typically seek to establish a sense of identity, that is, to think of themselves as possessing a distinct and unique character, of being people in their own right—distinct from their parents and siblings.

At this stage of development, personal identity is linked to and differentiated from the identity of parents and family in a special way. Often the social forces of the community, along with physiological changes, exert pressure on the adolescent to disengage (positive assessment of distance) from his or her family. Participation in school or work is expected, as is a social life outside the family. The expectation increases that the adolescent will have a life outside the family.

To some parents (and some children, too), however, surrendering closeness (distance negative) often comes hard. Parents may have difficulty changing their negative assessment of distance to a positive assessment. They cling to the *unconditional* belief that they must be close to their children. After regarding daughters and sons as children for so many years, it is difficult for some parents to start treating them as adults. So the relationship between adolescent and parents is often fraught with difficulties. The adolescent's search for an identity sometimes takes the form of a negative assessment of closeness to the parents.

Adolescents struggle to resolve their identification with their parents and to build from this identification a personal identity uniquely their own. The intellectual development of adolescents advances to a stage in which they can think in abstractions, form theories about what life is all about, and contemplate what the world might be rather than what it seems to be (Kagan and Segal, 1968). Often their thinking makes them critical of the values held by their parents. They begin to question their families' trait and relational assessments. "Why can't I date someone of a different religion or race?" "Why can't I buy the most expensive stereo set?" "How come I have to spend the holidays at home, when I want to be with my friends?" It is a time of groping and questioning, a time in which adolescents search for the values and beliefs that will guide their behavior for the major part of their life. It is exactly here that adolescents confront the challenge of assessing relations in an active, participatory way.

As the adolescent grows and moves out of the family circle, one of his or her major concerns is to reconcile differences in relational values. Consider a person who once, as an adolescent, leaned heavily on her parents' assessment that "it is important to be close to your family." Suppose that this assessment goes deep, that the person thinks of herself as belonging to her family. She interprets her mother's behavior. She interprets her father's behavior. She acts in relation to this interpretation. So she is a person belonging to Mother and Father, and she therefore acts out the part of being unconditionally close to her parents. This quality of closeness she feels to her parents is claimed with pride. She sees herself as loyal, protective, responsible, and responsive to the value of family togetherness.

Suppose this woman meets a man with whom she falls in love. She feels torn between her loyalty toward her parents and this newfound intimacy she feels with her boyfriend. He wants her to commit to the relationship. But if she gets close to him, she betrays the family value of togetherness. Confusion arises. So she deals with this problem by cutting off the relationship with her parents in an attempt to gain her independence and by doing that resolve the inconsistency.

The woman finds herself caught in an inconsistent context of opposing relational values. The category "closeness to family" limits her mindset to the notion that "family is mother and father." Therefore, "family closeness means being close to mother and father." "If I am close to boyfriend I am distant from family," and "if I am close to my family I am distant from my boyfriend." To resolve the problem she tries to eliminate the inconsistency by distancing herself from her family.

Reconciling opposing relational values does not end during young adulthood. For most adults, marriage means adjusting to another person's relational values. Consider the case of a couple. The husband grew up in a family where privacy was valued. The wife grew up in a family where everyone shared information and everyone knew everything about the others.

The husband assesses "closeness" negatively ("She is intrusive") and "distance" positively ("I like my privacy"). The wife, however, assesses closeness positively ("I like to share things with my husband") and distance negatively ("He is hiding something from me"). Therefore, the values they assign to closeness and distance, although consistent with their extended families' values, are inconsistent with the other's values.

Both the husband and the wife engage in behaviors that they consider appropriate and consistent with their extended families' values. "In the eyes of each of them the particular . . . behavior of the other is seen as that behavior that needs correction. For instance, the wife may have the impression that her husband is not open enough for her to know his position, what is going on in his head, what he is doing when he is away from home, etc. Quite naturally, she will, therefore, attempt to get the needed information by asking him questions, watching his behavior, and checking on him in a variety of other ways. If he considers her behavior as too intrusive, he is likely to withhold from her information which in and by itself would be quite harmless and irrelevant to disclose. . . . The less information he gives her, the more persistently she will seek it, and the more she seeks it, the less he will give her" (Watzlawick, Weakland, and Fisch, 1974,

p. 35). So the couple find themselves caught in a contentious interpersonal context stemming from opposing relational assessments.

It is probably clear at this point that each person comes to possess a set of relational assessments that constitutes his or her unique style. We have tried to show that maintaining one's identity of assessments is an ongoing dynamic process that evolves throughout the life cycle. Each day's experience calls for the consolidation of some aspects of one's assessments and changes of others. If it were a static world we lived in, our assessments might be static, too. But new things keep happening, and our assessments keep turning out in expected or unexpected ways (Kelly, 1955). Life always combines changes in inner conditions, which are the result of ongoing developmental processes, and changes in the milieu—the context. Often the interplay between these inner and outer changes generates inconsistencies and differences between relational values.

These examples illustrate that people do not always use flexibility when dealing with changes and inconsistencies. Rather, their assessments become like fixed, programmed values ("I must be close to my family"; "My wife should always respect my privacy"; "Sharing things with my husband is essential"). People get stuck in rigid, fixed assessment styles. They treat their assessments as though they were context-free—true despite changes in circumstances (Giacomo and Weissmark, 1992a, 1992b; Langer, 1989; Weissmark and Giacomo, 1994, 1995). They become blind to the notion that their assessments are actually based on conditional values. So problems may arise at any level of human functioning, including the individual level, the dyadic level, or the familial level. The reluctance to use one's flexibility, is, of course, one of the matters that confronts the psychotherapist in dealing with his or her patient.

The Passive-Observant Profile and the Active-Participatory Profile

When people get stuck in a fixed assessment style, they tend to present a *passive-observant profile* (P1), characterized by rigidity (unconditional assessments), detachment (external assessments), and ineffectiveness (reactive assessments).

Put somewhat differently, they tend to view their relationships as unconditional. That is to say, they believe that circumstances are unimportant. For example, the statement "I must be close to my family" shows that people assess the relationship independently of the circumstances.

They also tend to assess their relations in a *reactive* way. For example, the statement "No matter what I do he goes into my briefcase" shows that people feel unable to change the relationship.

And finally, they tend to assess their relations in an *external* way. For example, the statement "He is hiding something from me" shows that people do not feel responsible for the relationship.

By contrast, people who have a more adaptable assessment style tend to present an *active-participatory profile* (P2), characterized by flexibility (conditional assessments), involvement (internal assessments), and effectiveness (selective assessments).

Put somewhat differently, they tend to view their relationships as *conditional*. That is to say, they believe that circumstances are important. For example, the statement "He can go into my briefcase to leave me a gift" shows that people assess the circumstances of the relationship.

They also tend to assess their relations in a *selective* way. For example, the statement "I stop him from going into my briefcase" shows that people feel able to change the relationship.

And finally, they tend to assess their relations in an *internal* way. For example, the statement "I left my briefcase open" shows that people feel responsible for the relationship.

FINDINGS FROM THE ATTRIBUTION LITERATURE

There has been a great deal of research in the attribution literature showing the link between the passive-observant profile and causal attributions. Attribution theorists attempt to resolve how individuals answer such questions as "Why has Mary rejected me?" "Why have I failed?" "Why is Tom depressed?" The originator of this conceptual approach, Fritz Heider, and subsequent contributors were interested in causal issues of social behavior and personality.

Social and personality psychologists have fostered a voluminous literature devoted to causal explanations given for events ranging from achievements to social-relational phenomena. There is no need to review this prolific research activity because this has been done (see, for example, Weiner, 1990). However, a brief discussion of some of the findings seems useful because they suggest that causal assessments have cognitive, affective, interpersonal, and motivational effects that are characteristic of the passive-observant profile.

According to findings from the attribution theory of motivation and emotion (Weiner, 1985), retrospective judgments of the causes of one's achievement have motivational effects. Individuals, for example, who credit their successes to personal capabilities and their failures to insufficient *effort* will undertake difficult tasks and persist in the face of failure, because they see their outcomes as being influenced by how much effort they expend. In contrast, those who ascribe their failures to deficiencies in *ability* and their successes to situational factors will display low striving and give up readily when they encounter obstacles.

It was evident to attributional theorists that effort as a cause is different from ability. To make comparisons possible, attributional theorists identified characteristics of causes. For example, ability as a cause of an achievement is generally perceived as internal to the person, stable (enduring over time), global (appearing in a variety of settings), and uncontrollable (characteristic of one not able to volitionally alter the cause), whereas effort is generally perceived as external to the person, unstable (not lasting over time), specific (appearing in a specific setting), and controllable (characteristic of one who can volitionally alter the cause).

Many studies have demonstrated the relationship between causal characteristics, emotions, and behaviors. The emotions of anger and sympathy, for example, were shown to be determined in part by whether a cause is perceived as controllable. In this context controllability was linked with personal responsibility—given a controllable cause, the person was assumed to be held responsible. Many studies, for example, have shown that if hyperactive children are perceived as responsible for their misbehavior, anger and no help will follow. Another set of studies has shown that if depressed individuals are perceived as responsible for their depressive mood, anger and no help will follow. Still other studies have shown that if obese individuals are perceived as responsible for their obesity, anger and no help will follow. In contrast, when hyperactivity, depression, or obesity is attributed to uncontrollable factors (for instance, being inborn, neurological, chemical, or hormonal), pity, sympathy, and help will follow (Weiner, 1990).

Other studies have manipulated rather than observed control and have examined the effects of these manipulations on a variety of emotions, cognitions, and behaviors. In these studies control was defined by an animal's responses. An animal has control when a desired outcome's occurrence is dependent on the animal's responses. That is, the outcome will not occur without the animal's making some response to bring it about. It was believed that perceived independence between an animal's responses and forthcoming outcomes results in "learned helplessness." Initial studies by Seligman (1975) and others appeared to show that animals, when first given uncontrollable shock, exhibit little motivation to respond when these behaviors become instrumental to escaping. This syndrome of cognitive and motivational deficits was compared to symptoms exhibited by depressed humans. Indeed, later work with both animals and humans has shown that exposing animals or humans to uncontrollable aversive outcomes may be devastating and may even result in the organism's premature death. From this experimental research the idea was generated that certain causal attributions about ability might also be dysfunctional. Abramson, Seligman, and Teasdale (1978) suggested that attributing failure to uncontrollable internal causes that do not change over time (causal stability) and to causes that appear in a variety of settings (causal globality) were maladaptive. This pattern was anticipated to lead to the onset of depression. On the other hand, ascriptions of failures that are controllable, external, unstable, and specific were considered adaptive.

Other studies have examined the role of control in field settings. In these studies control was defined as the active belief that one has a choice. Stotland and Blumenthal (1964), for instance, studied the effects of choice on anxiety reduction. They told subjects that they were going to take several important ability tests. Half of the subjects were allowed to choose the order in which they wanted to take the tests, and half were told that the order was fixed. They found that subjects not given the choice were more anxious.

Although using a very different paradigm, Langer and Rodin (1977) also showed the importance of choice. In one experimental study residents of a nursing home were divided into an experimental and a control group. Those in the experimental group were encouraged to choose some of their daily activities. Those in the control group were not encouraged to make decisions for themselves but were told that the staff was there to help them. The results showed dramatic improvement for the group given more choices on various behavioral and emotional measures. The most striking discovery was that those in the experimental group had a lower mortality rate.

Other studies have examined the role of people's perceptions of their efficacy. According to this definition, people's sense of control is governed in part by their belief about their capabilities. People's beliefs in their capabilities affect how much stress and depression they experience in threatening situations as well as their level of motivation. "People who believe they can exercise control over potential threats do not conjure up apprehensive cognitions and, therefore, are not perturbed by them. But those who believe they cannot manage potential threats experience high levels of stress and anxiety arousal" (Bandura, 1989, p. 1177).

Taken together, these findings show that causal attributions influence cognitive, affective, behavioral, and interpersonal functioning. The causal characteristic that has received the most attention is controllability. Experts in the field have focused on various aspects of control in defining and studying what control is. Some have defined control as "a person's judgment about responsibility"; others have defined it as "a person making some response to cause an outcome" (that is, a person has control when a desired outcome's occurrence is dependent on the person's responses); others have defined it as the "active belief that one has a choice"; and finally others have defined it as "the belief that one can manage potential threats."

Thus there is reason to conclude that the construct of "controllability" is not simply a unidimensional phenomenon. Rather, the various definitions all appear to tap different aspects of the same phenomena. That is, the definitions draw on the different characteristics of the passive-observant profile described earlier. Whether control is defined as responsibility, responsivity, choice, or self-efficacy, the findings from the attribution literature demonstrate that when one's belief in control is threatened, the results are quite similar. The weaker the belief in controllability, the more likely the person will present a P1 profile characterized by rigid (unconditional), detached (external), and ineffective (reactive) assessments, which in turn affect thought patterns, determine motivational behaviors, and affect emotional functioning.

In the attribution literature, the dimensional characteristics (external, reactive, and unconditional) typical of the P1 profile are thought to be dysfunctional. This is especially evident in the attributional therapy literature. Together with the growth of attributional research, there has been a growing field of attributional therapy (see Forsterling, 1985, 1986). Attributional therapies are guided by the fundamental principle that causal ascriptions of controllability are more adaptive than causal ascriptions of uncontrollability. Attributional therapies have been, for the most part, confined to achievement-related contexts. For instance, attribution therapists presume that it is better for a person to ascribe failure to lack of effort (because effort is controllable) than to lack of ability (because ability is uncontrollable). The goal of attributional therapies, therefore, has been to substitute adaptive causal ascriptions for those that are dysfunctional, with the anticipation that this alteration will produce positive changes in behavior (Weiner, 1990).

Although there is much value to the principle that causal controllability is better than causal uncontrollability, for a thorough understanding of a person's assessment style we must recognize its dynamic, multidimensional aspects. This is important in a practical sense when we formulate explicit clinical intervention strategies. We can encourage people to think that depression, obesity, or hyperactivity is an uncontrollable condition; we can give them decisions to make; we can instruct them to attribute their failures to effort; and we can increase their belief in their own self-efficacy.

But if we encourage people to think they are not responsible for their depression (or obesity, or hyperactivity), are we discouraging self-initiated actions toward alleviating the problem? If we give people decisions to make, are ten choices too many or too few? If we teach people to attribute their failure to effort, and if we increase their belief in their self-efficacy, should we do so even in situations where they are lacking the ability to succeed? (For example, if an individual does not make the basketball team because she is too short, should we still encourage her to attribute her failure to effort and increase her belief in her self-efficacy?)

As researchers continue to explore the field, it has become apparent that a singularly positive or negative understanding of controllability is inadequate. Indeed, we can confirm this just by appealing to our everyday experience. Decreasing a person's sense of responsibility may imply that the problem is one that the person cannot control without outside aid. Giving a person too many alternatives may be overwhelming, and thus the alternatives will be ignored rather than inspire consideration and feelings of competence (Langer, 1983). Encouraging self-efficacy beliefs in situations where persons are lacking the ability to succeed may lead to the perception of no control and distinct feelings of inadequacy and frustration.

These dilemmas highlight both the positive and the negative consequences of equating the assessment of controllability with adaptive behavior (and, conversely, uncontrollability with dysfunctional behavior). In the real world in which we live, assessments of controllability are simultaneously positive with respect to some criteria and negative with respect to others.

Reciprocal Movement between the Passive-Observant Profile and the Active-Participatory Profile

In contrast to the attributional approach, which is guided by definitions that are static, unidimensional, and singularly positive or negative, the theory of assessing relations assumes that a person's assessment style is dynamic, multidimensional, and conditional. Whereas the attributional approach asserts that assessments of uncontrollability are dysfunctional, the theory of assessing relations presumes that all passive assessments (including the assessment of uncontrollability) are adaptive, depending on the circumstances. Put another way, the theory of assessing relations presumes that in some situations P1 assessments may be sufficient for effective functioning and at other times P2 assessments may be required. The theory of assessing relations is guided by the fundamental principle that there is reciprocal movement between the passive mode of assessment and the active mode of assessment. Both modes are necessary for adaptive functioning. This reciprocal movement is well described in Piaget's work on assimilation and accommodation.

According to Piaget, the two key terms that describe people's ability to adapt to changes are *assimilation* and *accommodation* (1947/1972). Assimilation is the process of incorporating new events (inconsistencies, incompatible values, developmental transformations, novel situations, new facts, and so on) into one's existing set of assessments. Conversely, accommodation is the process of modifying one's existing set of assessments when dealing with new events.

As a simple example (taken from Kagan and Segal, 1968), consider a young girl who has many toys. To these familiar toys we add a new one—a magnet. The girl's first impulse will be to assimilate the new toy into her assessment of her other toys; she may try to bang it like a hammer, throw it like a ball, or blow it like a horn. But once she realizes that the magnet has a new quality—the power to attract iron—she may accommodate her assessments of "toys" to include this previously unfamiliar fact. She now plays with the magnet according to her modified assessment that some toys are not designed to bang, throw, or make noise with but to attract metal. Thus, the girl actively alters her original assessment to fit the new event.

When children or adults accommodate their assessments to new events they are using the active-participatory mode. There are various ways in which people can actively accommodate their assessments to new events. We might call them (1) qualifying one's assessments (that is, making them conditional), (2) exceeding one's assessments, (3) reframing one's assessments, and (4) refining one's assessments. We shall examine each of these in turn.

Qualifying assessments refers to making one's assessments conditional. For instance, the category "closeness"-"distance" is not intrinsically either "good" or "bad." In some situations closeness may be good, and in other situations distance may be good. As described earlier, consider a young person who values her parents' assessment that "it is important to be close to your family." She experiences her first intimate relationship as a betrayal of her family's value of "togetherness." So she reacts to this conflict by unconditionally distancing herself from her parents. But there are more active-participatory ways of dealing with this conflict. She could, for instance, specify the conditions when she will be close (or distant from) her family and her boyfriend: "I want to stay close to my parents, but only if I can have my own life, too. So, I'll spend holidays with my parents, but weekends are for my boyfriend and me." Here she is qualifying her positive assessment of closeness by making it dependent on circumstances. Thus, when a person makes assessments conditional in an active-participatory way, he or she is considering the circumstances of the situation.

Exceeding assessments refers to transcending one's set of assessments. For instance, consider the case of the couple described earlier. Their conflict stems from different relational values. The husband assesses "closeness" negatively ("She is intrusive") and "distance" positively ("I like my privacy"). The wife assesses closeness positively ("I like to share things with my husband") and distance negatively ("He is hiding something from me"). Both of them are fixed on retaining their assessments. So they try to eliminate the conflict by blaming the other person (external) and by insisting the other change some behavior. But there are more active-participatory ways of dealing with this interpersonal conflict. The couple could, for instance, agree that getting along is more important than whether the other person is being intrusive or secretive. Both of them could agree to assess the new relation "compatibility" positively: "My wife and I think it is important to overlook our differences." "My husband and I like living a harmonious life." Thus, when people exceed their assessments in an active-participatory way, they are transcending their set of existing assessments.

Reframing assessments refers to changing the values of one's assessments. As noted earlier, relations have contrasting poles that can be assessed either negatively or positively. In the example cited before, suppose the wife discovers that her husband was not trying to hide anything from her. Her negative assessment of distance ("secretive") may change to the positive assessment "private." Also, suppose the husband discovers that his wife was asking him questions because she was genuinely interested in how he spent his time when they were apart. His negative assessment of closeness ("intrusive") may change to the positive assessment "caring." When people change the values they give to their assessments in an active-participatory way, they are reframing their set of assessments.

Refining assessments refers to expanding one's set of assessments. For instance, consider our earlier example of the young girl who has many toys and receives a new one—a magnet. This new toy produces an unfamiliar, conflictual experience. So the girl's first response is to limit her assessment of toys to include only those that she is already familiar with: toys that bang, throw, or make noise. Later, however, she chooses a more active way of dealing with the event. She enlarges her assessment of toys to include ones that also attract metal. Thus, when people enlarge their assessments in an active-participatory way, they are refining their set of existing assessments rather than limiting them.

We can see, then, that accommodation involves modifying one's existing set of assessments when dealing with new events. This can be done in different ways. People can make their assessments conditional. They can transcend them altogether. They can reframe their assessments by altering their values. Or they can refine their assessments. In all these instance, we can say that people are using the active-participatory mode to modify their assessments.

Sometimes, however, people do not use the active-participatory mode. They get stuck in rigid, fixed assessments and they adapt to new events in passive-observant ways. When people assimilate new events into their existing assessments, they are making assessments in a passive-observant way. There are many ways in which this can be done. If we compare the active ways listed above to the passive ways, we might call the passive ways un-qualifying one's assessments—that is, making them unconditional, retaining one's set of assessments, sticking to the values of one's assessments, and limiting one's assessments (Giacomo and Weissmark, 1992a; Weissmark and Giacomo, 1994, 1995).

Often, there is tension between the passive process of assimilation and the more active process of accommodation. Initially, assimilation and accommodation are opposed to each other, since assimilation is conservative and tends to subordinate new events to the person's set of assessments as it is, whereas accommodation is the source of changes and bends the person's assessments to the new events. But if in their rudiments these two processes are antagonistic, according to Piaget, it is precisely the role of mental life and intelligence to coordinate them (1972).

This coordination, according to Piaget, presupposes no special force of organization, since from the beginning assimilation and accommodation are inseparable. They are the two poles of an interaction between a person and the new events he or she must face. Such an interaction presupposes a dynamic equilibrium between the two tendencies of opposing poles. That is, there is reciprocal movement between the two processes. Accommodating new events is extended eventually into assimilation. It is a matter of conserving new assessments and of reconciling them with the old ones.

An increasingly close interconnection thus tends to be established between the two processes. Sometimes, however, the relation between assimilation and accommodation loses its mutual dependence. When this occurs assimilation may prevail. And the reciprocal movement between passive-observant ways and active-participatory ways gets stuck.

According to Kagan (1989), the inability to shift from a passive-observant state to an active-participatory state may be due to any number of reasons including biological, social, or environmental factors. There is, for instance, considerable evidence that one biological difference among people is the sensitivity of the autonomic nervous system (ANS) to new events. Some of us react to unfamiliar, novel situations with restraint (and a heart rate that is unusually high), while others act spontaneously (and by only a small change in heart rate), as though the distinction between the familiar and the novel were of small psychological consequence. A person who is more easily aroused by novelty requires a longer time to recover, and thus the time required to assimilate such experiences is greater (Kagan, 1989). So, accommodative activity may be delayed or even avoided altogether. When this occurs, the relation between assimilation and accommodation loses its mutual dependence, and shifting from passive-observant ways to active-participatory ways may become impaired.

Whatever the cause, the net result is always the same—a loss of the flexibility to shift from the passive-observant mode to the active-participatory mode. When a person becomes unable to move from passive ways to active ways, conflict, discomfort, or pathology may follow. It is here that the therapist may help. The therapist's task is to create a context that reestablishes the reciprocal movement between the passive process of assimilation and the active process of accommodation. As we explore the therapeutic process further in the next chapter, we will examine how the therapist accomplishes this task. We will ask what therapist actions contribute to helping patients shift from a passive-observant profile to an active-participatory profile.

Summing Up

We began this chapter by showing that relational assessments are multidimensional assessments. Three crucial dimensions on which relations are assessed are the unconditional-conditional, the external-internal, and the reactive-selective. The evaluation of these dimensions bears on the meaning people give to their relational assessments. For example, it makes a great deal of difference whether a person feels powerless to change a relationship (reactive) or whether a person believes he or she can effect changes through his or her own efforts (selective).

We pointed out that the assessments a person gives to a relation define for him or her what he or she feels, says, and does. If, for instance, you define your friend's behavior as intrusive, you might get angry and tell her to mind her own business. Your angry feelings reflect the negative pattern of values you give to the relation "intrusion," which in turn guides your behavioral response of telling your friend to mind her business. Your cognitive evaluation ("I don't like people intruding"), your affective response ("I am angry"), and your behavioral action ("Mind your business") all share a common currency, namely, the negative assessment of the relation "intrusive."

The claim that emotions involve a cognitive assessment of a particular relation is different from saying that the contribution of cognition is a conscious process. You may get angry with your friend for snooping around your desk, yet you may be unaware that you are assessing intrusion negatively. Somehow, without deliberate awareness people automatically assess the value of their relationships.

The point is clearly recognized by authors of literature. Writers do not always have to state what emotions a character is experiencing because the described situation contains the relational assessments. This suggests that writers use an implicit theory that individual emotions can be specified in terms of relational assessments that are sufficient to produce them. Shakespeare, for example, can reliably produce in readers an awareness of Othello's affective state by portraying a situation that challenges Othello's assessment of "loyalty."

Empirical research has produced support for this implicit theory by showing strong connections among emotion, behavior, and the assessment of relations. Among the relations studied intensively is the relation "attachment" (or closeness-distance). The procedure of briefly separating an infant from its mother has been a key experimental method in the study of attachment. Using this experimental method, researchers have shown that babies between twelve and fifteen months assess the relation "closeness" positively and the relation "distance" negatively. When an infant is separated from the individual to whom it is attached, he or she performs a set of behaviors and exhibits emotional distress.

As an infant matures his or her relational assessments continue to evolve. Eventually the child's assessments are those by which he or she maintains his or her individuality. As the adolescent moves out from the family circle, one of his or her major concerns is to reconcile differences in relational values. This need does not end during young adulthood. For most adults, marriage is a time when they must adjust to another person's relational values.

We tried to point out that assessing relations is an ongoing dynamic process that evolves throughout the life cycle. Life involves changes that may generate inconsistencies or differences between values. People do not always use flexibility when dealing with life's changes. They may treat their assessments as though they were context-free—true despite changes in circumstances. They may become blind to the notion that their assessments are actually based on conditional values.

When people get stuck in a fixed assessment style, they present a passive-observant profile, characterized by unconditional, external, and reactive assessments. By contrast, people who have a more flexible assessment style present an active-participatory profile, characterized by conditional, internal, and selective assessments.

Findings from attributional research suggest that causal assessments have cognitive, affective, behavioral, and interpersonal effects that are characteristics of the passive-observant profile. The causal characteristic that has received the most attention is controllability. Whether control is responsibility, responsivity, choice, or self-efficacy, the findings from the attribution literature show that when one's belief in control is threatened the results are quite similar. The weaker the belief in controllability the more likely the person will present a passive-observant profile.

In contrast to the attributional approach, which is guided by the view that passive assessments are dysfunctional, the theory of assessing relations assumes both modes are necessary for adaptive functioning. The theory of assessing relations is guided by the principle that there is reciprocal movement between the passive mode of assessment and the active mode of assessment.

This reciprocal movement is well described in Piaget's work on assimilation and accommodation. When people assimilate events into their existing set of assessments, they are treating new events in a passive-observant manner. By contrast, when people accommodate or modify their assessments to meet new events, they are treating new events in an active-participatory manner. A close interconnection is established between the two processes. Sometimes, however, the relation between assimilation and accommodation loses its mutual dependence. When this occurs the reciprocal movement between passive-observant ways and active-participatory ways gets stuck.

In chapter 5, we will examine how therapists help patients shift their assessments from a passive-observant profile to an active-participant profile. We will ask what therapist actions facilitate shifts in patients' assessments. We then present statistical data to show there are specific therapist behaviors that can facilitate or impede changes in patients' assessments, which, in turn, predict treatment outcome.

In presenting these data, we will offer an operational definition of psychotherapy precise enough to specify therapists' behaviors. It is also flexible enough to describe the different ways that psychotherapy is actually practiced. This feature, we hope, will help narrow the gap between the research and the practice of psychotherapy.

5

Measuring Therapeutic Interactions

What Does the Psychotherapist Do?

In chapter 4 we examined how people use relations to organize their every-day experiences. We pointed out that assessing relations is an ongoing, dynamic process that evolves throughout the life cycle. People are continuously assessing their relationships with others while simultaneously modifying these assessments during ordinary interactions.

For instance, suppose a woman assesses the relation "intrusion" negatively. If she discovers that her husband went into her briefcase, she may react angrily because she believes that her husband's act was intrusive. But if she later discovers that her husband was putting a gift in her briefcase, her angry response may change to one of gratitude because she modifies her assessment and perceives the relationship to be intimate rather than intrusive.

This example shows how people assess and change their relationships, here from intrusiveness ("He is very nosy") to intimacy ("He and I are very close"). Three crucial dimensions on which relations are assessed are the internal-external, the selective-reactive, and the conditional-unconditional. Internal-external is about assuming responsibility for a relation. Selective-reactive describes the ability to change a relationship. Conditional-unconditional refers to the circumstances of a relationship.

People use these relations and dimensions to organize and assess their experiences in their everyday life, and as described above, they are modifiable during ordinary interactions. In psychotherapy, the relations that people ordinarily assess are potentially the sites for clinical interventions. Psychotherapy is operationally defined as a process of systematically inducing changes in the way people organize their experiences along dimensions and relations. A therapeutic alliance is created when a therapist establishes the conditions that help patients to change their assessments in a systematic way. The therapeutic alliance is not by itself curative. Rather, it is an ingredient that makes it possible for the patient to follow treatment (Bordin, 1980).

To create the conditions for treatment, effective therapists use three operations: they encourage patients to assess relationships when describing their difficulties; they match the relationships appraised by the patients; and they induce patients to take responsibility (*internal*) for the relations they assess, to effect changes (*selective*) in their relationships, and to consider the circumstances (*conditional*). In essence, then, effective therapists use these operations to create a context for helping patients to engage in an inquiry that will produce self-change.

When therapists undertake psychotherapy with a patient, they can apply these operations by approaching their task from many viewpoints. There are many different techniques, therefore, that therapists can use to create the conditions for treatment. For instance, cognitive therapists use techniques such as eliciting automatic thoughts and identifying maladaptive assumptions, whereas interpersonal therapists use techniques such as reassurance and improvement of interpersonal communication. However different these techniques may seem, they share a common function, namely, readjusting a person's assessments. That is to say, despite differences in technique and theory, at the level of practice therapists use the same operation to get patients to readjust their assessments. The many ways (that is, techniques) of using an operation are all vehicles for engaging a patient in a moving inquiry that is the very process of psychotherapy (Havens, 1986; Kelly, 1955).

Consider as an analogy research on student satisfaction conducted at Harvard (Light, 1990). Students have clear ideas about what kinds of courses they are satisfied with. When asked, students list three crucial features: (1) immediate and detailed feedback, (2) high demands and standards, and (3) frequent evaluations.

Faculty interested in improving teaching effectiveness can find many ways to give feedback to students, to maintain high standards, and to give frequent evaluations. Concerning the first feature, they could, for example, meet individually with students to discuss their work, they could give them written feedback, or they could have students read their work to each other during class. These different ways are vehicles for the same function—giving students feedback—which in turn is part of the educational experience. In brief, the point we want to stress is, as Freud puts it, "There are many ways and means of practicing psychotherapy. All that lead to recovery are good" (1904/1959, p. 252).

Despite differences in viewpoints and techniques between different schools of therapy, at the level of practice the dynamics of the therapeutic process are similar. Put in colloquial terms, effective therapists induce patients to accept positive points of view: "You're responsible"; "You can select"; "Circumstances matter" (H. Senger, personal communication, 1994).

Although different schools of psychotherapy place different emphasis on what changes should be called emotional growth, most schools emphasize that improvement is related to the capacity of patients to take responsibility for their behavior. Responsibility can be defined as the capacity of individuals to hold themselves fully accountable for what they do, think, or feel. Responsible individuals accept their behavior as their own (internal) rather than seeing themselves as passive victims of their environment (reactive and external). They believe they have choice in deciding their behavior, can control their actions, and can exercise a certain amount of will (selective). They also believe they can adapt to changing circumstances (conditional).

In summary, people use relations and dimensions to organize their experiences. People use language to express these relations and dimensions. The statement "You are always telling me what to do" expresses the relation "dominance" and the dimensions "unconditional" and "external." Every act of organizing experiences is a way of assessing choice and responsibility. Thus, the possibility for change rests in each person's self-assessment process.

In therapy, the relations and dimensions that people ordinarily assess are potentially the sites for clinical intervention. A patient-therapist interaction is therapeutic when a therapist creates conditions to help patients change their assessments. The combined therapeutic operations—induction of relational assessments and transformations from external to internal, reactive to selective, and unconditional to conditional assessments—result in a tendency to maximize an active-participatory profile in the patient (from a P1 to a P2). The Harvard Psychotherapy Coding Method operationalizes these therapist operations.

The Harvard Psychotherapy Coding Method

The Harvard Psychotherapy Coding Method (HPCM) was developed during the Harvard Psychotherapy Research Project, which began in 1988 following a five-year period of pilot work. During the pilot study, video-tapes of expert therapists were analyzed to develop common principles of practice (Giacomo and Weissmark, 1986, 1987). By focusing on therapists' actions at the level of practice, we identified unifying principles that cut across different schools of therapy. The analyses from these pilot studies suggest that therapy is an interactional process in which an effective thera-pist encourages a patient to assess relationships, to make choices, and to assume responsibility for change.

The Harvard project was designed to extend the pilot study. The first task was to develop a measure that operationalizes therapists' and patients' behaviors. Since the overall aim of the project was to develop a measure that was predictive of treatment outcome and clinically relevant, the vari-ables needed to measure aspects of therapists' behaviors that could poten-tially be modified during training and aspects of patients' behaviors that could potentially be changed during treatment (Giacomo and Weissmark, 1992a, 1992b; Weissmark and Giacomo, 1994). The operational defini-tions of the variables to be described below summarize the coding variables of the HPCM, which is designed to measure aspects of therapists' behav-iors that facilitate or impede progress in therapy and aspects of patients' behaviors that shift or remain stable during treatment.

CODING VARIABLES

The Harvard Psychotherapy Coding Method measures the way partici-pants organize their experiences during therapy (Weissmark and Giacomo, 1988). The variables consist of patient variables and therapist variables.

Patient Variables

People continuously assess their relationships with others—for instance, intimacy ("My mother and I are very close"), intrusiveness ("He comes over without calling first"), and dominance ("He orders me around"). As described above, the three crucial dimensions on which relationships are assessed are the internal-external, the reactive-selective, and the condi-tional-unconditional. Internal-external is about assuming responsibility for a relationship. Statements that show a person feels responsible for a rela-

Table 5.1 Patient Variables

Variables	Examples
Relational	"We are close."
Internal	"I don't want to get involved."
External	"He doesn't want to get involved."
Reactive	"No matter what I do, he backs off."
Selective	"I stop him from backing off."
Conditional	"I will get close only to people I trust."
Unconditional	"I never want to be in a close relationship."

tionship are internal; those that show a person does not feel responsible are external. Reactive-selective describes the ability to change a relationship. Statements that show a person is unable to change a relationship are reactive; those that show a person believes she can change a relationship are selective ("I stop him from backing off"). Conditional-unconditional refers to the circumstances of a relationship. Statements that show a person believes a relationship depends on circumstances are conditional; those that show a person believes a relationship is independent of the circumstances are unconditional. Table 5.1 presents examples of the patient variables.

The coding method of the HPCM provides binary ratings for extracting the relational-material variable embedded in a patient's discourse. It provides numerical ratings for identifying thirty relations. In addition, the system provides binary ratings for coding the dimensions internal-external, selective-reactive, and conditional-unconditional assessments.

Therapist Variables

The relations and dimensions people use to assess their experiences are modifiable during ordinary interactions. For instance, a person's anger about feeling intruded on may change to gratitude if that person assesses "intrusion" conditionally (for example, a friend comes to visit without calling first to bring you a birthday gift). The change from anger to gratitude reflects a change in the assessment of the relation "intrusion" from unconditional ("I expect you to call before visiting") to conditional ("I didn't know you wanted to bring me a gift"). A person's assessment along the three dimensions is bidirectional (that is, shifting from conditional to unconditional or vice versa).

In therapy, the relations and dimensions that people ordinarily assess become the potential sites for clinical interventions. The HPCM operationally defines therapy as a process of systematically inducing changes in the way patients organize their experiences along relationships and dimensions. The task of a therapist is to facilitate changes in the way patients organize their experiences. These changes are induced by systematically operating on the patient variables (relationships and dimensions). For example, a therapist may induce a patient to change his or her assessment from external ("My friends are intrusive") to internal ("I drive them away"); from reactive ("I can't get close to anyone") to selective ("I can distinguish between closeness and intrusion"); and from unconditional ("People are always intrusive") to conditional ("Sometimes people just want to be close and are not intrusive").

Therapists induce changes along the patient variables by using three therapist variables: relational-material, inducers-noninducers, and matching—not matching. The relational-material variable refers to the assessment of relationships and attributes. Some examples of therapist statements that assess material attributes are "How old are you?" "Does anyone in the family have a history of depression?" "When did your problem begin?" Some examples of therapist statements that assess relations are "Is she intrusive?" "Do you feel close to your grandmother?" "Do you resent your wife taking charge?"

The inducers-noninducers variable describes the therapist-patient interaction. Therapist statements that elicit shifts in assessments from a patient are inducers. Some examples of inducers are "What can you do to stop him from being intrusive?" "Would you love him if he stood up to you?" Therapist statements that instruct a patient are noninducers. Some examples of instructive statements are "You have to move out." "You must not tolerate that behavior."

The matching—not matching variable is about identifying a relationship embedded in a patient's statement. Therapist statements that identify the same relationship a patient assesses are matched. Therapist statements that identify another relationship or no relationship are not matched. Table 5.2 shows examples of the therapist variables. It includes examples of inducers along each patient dimension.

The HPCM provides binary ratings for extracting the relational-material variable embedded in a therapist's discourse. It provides numerical ratings for identifying thirty relations. These binary and numerical ratings are the same as those used for rating patient statements. Also, the coding method includes binary ratings for coding the inducer-noninducer dimension. Matching is coded by checking whether the relationship extracted

Table 5.2 Therapist Variables

Variables	Examples
Material	"When did the problem begin?"
Relational	"Is he intrusive?"
Inducers	
Internal	"What do you do when he is intrusive?"
External	"How does he intrude?"
Reactive	"Do his intrusions make you feel helpless?"
Selective	"How do you stop him from intruding?"
Unconditional	"Do you think he will ever stop intruding?"
Conditional	"In what ways does he respect your privacy?"
Matching	P:* "I hate it when he comes over without calling first."
	T:* "Are you saying that you feel intruded on?"
Not matching	P: "I hate it when he comes over without calling first."
	T: "Have you always felt that way?"

*P = patient. T = therapist.

from a therapist's statement matches the relationship used by the patient in the prior statement.

RELIABILITY

In previous studies, the HPCM was used by one of the authors and an additional coder to code sixty transcripts (Giacomo and Weissmark, 1992a, 1992b; Weissmark and Giacomo, 1994). The second coder, who was clinically inexperienced, was trained by reading the HPCM, trying several standard practice cases, and receiving instructions from the authors. Ratings on these training cases were discussed to calibrate the judges. After eight weeks of training, the second coder, blind to the research hypotheses, independently coded a portion of the transcript. Random spot reliability checks of both coders were made periodically by having both coders unknowingly code the same transcript. Interrater agreement for all coding categories was moderate to high (kappa ranged from .70 to .81). Both coders were blind to the classification of successful and unsuccessful treatment outcome and were unaware they were coding a reliability transcript. This provides a reasonable demonstration of the absence of bias in the authors' ratings.

VALIDITY STUDIES

The HPCM was used in previous studies to test the method's predictive validity. Briefly, a total of fifteen therapists and thirty patients were included in the studies. The thirty therapeutic dyads were drawn from the Vanderbilt II psychotherapy research project (Henry et al., 1993). Dyad selection was structured to produce two equal groups (n = 15) based on patient outcome measures used in the Vanderbilt study. The outcome data from the Vanderbilt study consisted of pre-post residual change scores that were calculated on the SCL 90-R Global Severity Index (GSI) and the Global Outcome Ratings (GOR) made by the patient after therapy. These outcome measures were independent of the HPCM coding categories.

Participating patients were comparable to general psychiatric outpatients, as indicated by intake scores on the GSI. The two outcome groups were statistically equivalent on the GSI measure at intake. All patients were judged to have significant interpersonal difficulties and qualified for a *Diagnostic and Statistical Manual of Mental Disorders* Axis I or Axis II diagnosis as determined by a clinician using a computerized rating version of the National Institute of Mental Health (NIMH) Diagnostic Interview Schedule. There were no statistical differences between the two outcome groups on Axis I, Axis II, Axis IV, and Axis V diagnosis. The mean age of patients was forty-one (they ranged from twenty-six to sixty-four years); 77.5 percent were female, 48.8 percent were married, 25 percent were divorced, 17.5 percent were single, 3.7 percent were separated, and 5 percent were widowed. The mean level of education was three years of college. Patients were assigned on a random basis to participating therapists who were self-described psychodynamically oriented psychiatrists and clinical psychologists with a minimum of two years' full-time postinternship or postresidency experience. The fifteen therapists in the Vanderbilt study were aged twenty to fifty. Of these, eleven were male. Eight were licensed psychologists, and seven were psychiatrists. Therapies consisted of weekly fifty-minute meetings for a maximum of twenty-five sessions and were conducted with no intrusions by the research staff.

Transcripts of an early (session 3) and a late session (session 16) for each case were coded using the HPCM. Session 3 was selected so the hypotheses about the therapist predictive variables could be tested by an early session in treatment. Session 16 was selected so the hypotheses concerning the patient variables could be tested by process variations that may have occurred during treatment.

Hypotheses

The hypotheses entertained in the validity studies dealt with the relationship between patients' behaviors and treatment outcome and therapists' interventions and treatment outcome. Although one speaks of "patient variables" as separate from "therapist variables," each variable includes both sides, as described below in the coding procedure. For example, "matching" includes a therapeutic intervention that is possible only if a patient assesses a relation. Conversely, the assessment of a relation is guided by a therapeutic intervention. The inherent dynamic quality of the therapeutic interaction is preserved by the interactive nature of the HPCM coding categories.

Specifically, regarding the patient variables, we predicted the following: (1) in cases of successful therapy there will be significant changes from beginning to end of treatment in the patients' assessments from external to internal, from reactive to selective, and from unconditional to conditional; (2) in cases of unsuccessful therapy, the patients' assessments along the dimensions external-internal, reactive-selective, and unconditional-conditional will remain unchanged across treatment time.

Regarding the therapist variables, it was predicted that (1) in cases of successful therapy, the therapists will induce their patients to assess their situation along relations in more instances than those therapists who conducted unsuccessful therapy; (2) in cases of unsuccessful therapy, the therapist will use noninducers and will assess the patients' situation along material attributes significantly more than therapists who conducted successful therapy; and (3) in cases of successful therapy, the therapists will match the relations assessed by the patients significantly more than the therapists who conducted unsuccessful therapy.

Results

As predicted, the results showed that patients of a successful therapy were more likely to shift their assessments from external to internal, from reactive to selective, and from unconditional to conditional, whereas patients of an unsuccessful therapy were more likely to maintain external, reactive, and unconditional assessments. In brief, the data showed that at the beginning of treatment, patients' assessments, on the average, were external, reactive, and unconditional. During treatment, patients who shifted their assessments from external to internal, $t(14) = 3.465$, $p = .0038$, from reactive to selective, t(14) = 5.593, p = .0001, and unconditional to conditional, t(14) = 3.608, p = .0029, were more likely to rate their therapy as successful and improve (Giacomo and Weissmark, 1992a, 1992b).

Also as predicted, the results showed that therapists of a successful treatment, when interacting with patients, (a) produced significantly more statements that matched the relational assessments contained in the patients' statements and that induced the patients to reassess their situation along the patient variables and (b) assessed in terms of relations the patients' situations. By contrast, therapists of an unsuccessful therapy, when interacting with patients, were more likely to use statements that do not match the relational assessments of patients and that instruct patients and to assess in terms of material attributes the patients' situations. In brief, the data showed that the HPCM therapist variables are predictive of treatment outcome: matching, t(14) = 5.179, p = .0001; inducers, t(14) = 6.529, p = .0001; relational, t(14) = 5.500, p = .0001. Therapists of a successful therapy encouraged patients to assess relationships when describing their difficulties. They matched the relationships appraised by the patients, and they induced changes in the patients' assessments of the three dimensions from external to internal, from reactive to selective, and from unconditional to conditional.

Finally, the results showed that the therapeutic index variable accounted for 85 percent of the variance in the classification of treatment outcome as successful or unsuccessful (Giacomo and Weissmark, 1992a; Weissmark and Giacomo, 1994). The interpretation of these findings is subject, of course, to the limitations of all correlational research. The results provided no information regarding causality in the relation between outcome and the HPCM variables.

PROCEDURE

The procedure for using the HPCM involves two phases. The first phase consists of coding each therapist and patient statement (uninterrupted speeches) along the single-variables codes of the HPCM. The second phase consists of calculating the index for each therapist statement. A weight is assigned to each single therapeutic variable using a point system.

To illustrate the HPCM procedure, we have selected for presentation transcripts of segments from two family therapy sessions. Multiple raters were used to evaluate and ensure the reliability of observations made using the HPCM. Raters were chosen from among psychology graduate students.

The first segment is from a transcript of a consultation session that Minuchin conducted, and the second segment is from a transcript of a consultation that Nagy conducted. The cases were chosen to highlight the application of the HPCM to different theoretical schools (the structural and the contextual school).

Phase 1

Case 1 is taken from a family consultation session that Minuchin conducted while the mother was in the hospital because of a suicide attempt. The segment begins in the middle of an exchange between Minuchin and the father.

During the coding procedure the coders number each statement in the transcript (see table 5.3). For example

Case 1

265 THERAPIST (*to father*): How old are you?
266 FATHER: Forty-four.
267 THERAPIST (*to mother*): How old are you?
268 MOTHER: Forty.
269 THERAPIST: He's older than you?
270 MOTHER: Uh.
271 THERAPIST: Do you like your men young?
272 MOTHER: No.
273 THERAPIST: Why did you marry an adolescent?
274 MOTHER: I don't know.
275 THERAPIST: Why do you keep him like that?
276 MOTHER: I don't.
277 THERAPIST: Ahhh. That is a question. Is he an adolescent, or do you like him like that?
278 MOTHER: I hate him like that. Nothing you do changes him. You can't get through to him. It's like talking to a stone.
279 THERAPIST: But are you certain you could survive, that you could be married to a real man?

The coder then reads the transcripts and codes every statement made by the patient and the therapist. Each statement is coded along the variables just described. The results of the codings are entered onto a coding sheet that contains columns for each variable coded. The columns include the statement number, the speaker (patient or therapist), and the following dimensions: external-internal (0–1); reactive-selective (0–1); unconditional-

Table 5.3 Patient-Therapist Interactions

					Case 1			
No.	Speaker	Int.	Reac.	Cond.	Ind.	Mat./Rel.	Relationship	Match	Index
278	Mother	0	0	0	–	1	30	–	–
279	Therapist	1	1	1	1	1	20	0	5
					Case 2			
No.	Speaker	Int.	Reac.	Cond.	Ind.	Mat./Rel.	Relationship	Match	Index
55	Husband	0	0	0	–	1	6	–	–
56	Therapist	0	–	–	1	1	6	1	4

conditional (0–1); instructing-inducing (0–1); material-relational (0–1); relationship (01 to 30); and match—not match (1–0).

In case 1, therapist's statement number 265 ("How old are you?"), patient's statement number 266, therapist's statement number 267, patient's statement number 268, and therapist's statements numbers 269 and 271 all assess attributes and were coded as material (0). Also, therapist's statements numbers 265, 267, 269, and 271 all ask the patient factual information and were coded as noninducers (0).

Therapist's statement number 273 asks the patient to consider why she decided to marry an immature, "adolescent" man. It was coded as internal (1) and selective (1), containing the relationship (1) "rawness" (26). Therapist's statement number 275 asks the patient to consider how she may be contributing to maintaining her husband's immature behavior ("Why do you keep him like that?"). It was coded as internal (1) and selective (1), containing the relationship (1) "stationarity" (30). Therapist's statement number 277 continues to ask the patient to assess her role in maintaining her husband's immature behavior. It was coded as internal and (1) selective (1), containing the relationship "rawness" (26).

Patient's statement number 278 includes the evaluation of the relation "stationarity" (she perceives that her husband will not change). Also, the evaluation is unconditional ("I hate him like that"), reactive ("Nothing you do changes him"), and external ("It's like talking to a stone"). It was coded as an external (0), reactive (0), and unconditional (0) evaluation of the relationship (1) stationarity (30).

Therapist's statement number 279 shows the evaluation of the relation "maturity" (a real man). The evaluation is internal (1) ("Are you . . . ?"), selective (1) ("married to a real man"), and conditional (1) (if he were a real man). The statement also represents a therapeutic inducer (1) from external to internal, from unconditional to conditional, and from reactive to selective. Also, it was coded as relational (1), containing the relationship "maturity" (20) that does not match (0) the patient's previous evaluation of the relation "stationarity" (30) (see table 5.3).

Case 2 is taken from a consultation session that Nagy conducted with a couple who were in therapy because of a behavioral problem with their daughter. The segment begins in the middle of an exchange between Nagy and the husband. During phase 1 the statements in the following segment of the transcript were numbered:

Case 2

52 THERAPIST: Was that behavior a pattern?

53 HUSBAND: Yes, in a way, yes.

54 THERAPIST: What was the pattern? How can we learn from it?

55 HUSBAND: In a sense, my own feeling is no matter what I'd say about a situation like that or feel about it, it wouldn't have any influence on the final outcome anyway. So my own input wouldn't be relevant. It wouldn't be decisive.

56 THERAPIST: Why is it so? What is the explanation? I hear you are saying you put your best reasoning into something and you make a recommendation, a suggestion, and it is being ignored?

Therapist's statements numbers 52 and 54 ask the patient for factual information ("Was that behavior a pattern?" "What was the pattern?") and were coded as material (0) and as noninducers (0). Patient's statement number 55 shows the evaluation of the relationship (1) "influencelessness" (6) (he perceives that whatever he does lacks effect). Also, the evaluation is unconditional (0) ("no matter what I'd say . . .") and reactive (0) ("So my own input wouldn't be . . ."). Therapist's statement number 56 shows the evaluation of the relationship (1) "influencelessness" (6) ("you make a . . . suggestion, and it is being ignored") that matches (1) the relationship evaluated by the patient. Also, it was coded as external (0) ("and it is being ignored") (see table 5.3).

Phase 2

The successive statements coded in phase 1, as illustrated above, resulted in a set of sequentially recorded data that consisted of strings of categorical data. As such, the data can be represented in a time-frame format (Bakeman and Gottman, 1986). Each "frame" includes the codes that co-occurred during that particular therapist statement. For example, the coding of the therapist's statement 279 resulted in a frame that includes the string [1 1 1 1 1 0] (see table 5.3).

During phase 2 of the coding procedure, the codes are scaled on a multi-dimensional index (Weissmark and Giacomo, 1994). This index measures the impact of a therapist's statements on the therapeutic process. The different degrees of effectiveness are related to the types of dimensions assessed by the therapist.

At one extreme there is a high-interactive profile. It is characterized by a therapist who induces a patient to assess relationships and shift assessments and is sensitive to the relationships assessed by a patient. At the other extreme of the continuum there is a low-interactive profile. It is characterized by a therapist who instructs changes in a patient, does not induce a patient to assess relationships or shift assessments, and is not sensitive to the relationships assessed by the patient. The therapeutic index quantifies these patterns along a continuum.

The therapeutic index is computed by transforming the strings of categorical data into quantitative data. The transformation was done by using the following weights for each coding category:

1. If the therapist's statement contained an inducer and matched the patient's statement = +3
2. If the therapist's statement contained an inducer along a relational parameter = +2
3. If the therapist's statement contained the dimension internal, selective, or conditional = +1
4. If the therapist's statement contained no evaluation = 0
5. If the therapist's statement contained an external, reactive, or unconditional evaluation = −1
6. If the therapist's statement contained a noninducer = −2
7. If the therapist's statement contained a material parameter = −3

The weights were created by using a scale with zero in the middle, three weight values with positive signs, and three values with negative signs. Thus the weights have two components—their signs and their absolute values. The selection of the signs was based on the data described earlier. The poles of the therapeutic variables—relational, matching, and inducing—were assigned positive signs, and the nonrelational (material), nonmatching, and instructing were assigned negative signs. Similarly, the poles "internal," "selective," and "conditional" were assigned positive signs and the poles "external," "reactive," and "unconditional" were assigned negative signs. Following Gottman, Markman, and Notarius (1977), the absolute weight values were arbitrarily selected. Clinical experience and pilot work suggested how the therapist variables can be ordered in increasing order of effectiveness. The assessment of relations that matches the patient's has the highest absolute value, followed by inducing and the assessment of dimensions. One strength of the therapeutic index, however, is that it permits an investigator to test the predictability of other weight systems.

The coders reviewed the coding sheets and assigned the appropriate weights to the strings that co-occurred during each therapist's statement. The therapeutic value of each therapist's statement was then calculated by adding the weights. The therapeutic value of each statement ranged from a maximum of 8 to a minimum of –8. For example, the string [1 1 1 1 1 0] for statement 279 shows that the therapist statement included [2 (inducer along a relational parameter unmatched) + 1 (internal) + 1 (selective) + 1 (conditional)] and has a value of 5 (see table 5.3).

Studies have shown (Weissmark and Giacomo, 1994) that the therapeutic index was a significant predictor of treatment outcome ($r = .92$, $p < .0001$). Treatment outcome was more likely to be successful if the therapist had a high mean therapeutic index. The prediction about treatment outcome was not only significant statistically but also meaningful in magnitude by means of the binomial effect size display (BESD). This procedure, described in detail by Rosenthal and Rubin (1982), gives practical meaning to an effect size index and to research findings in general by showing that improvements in treatment success rates are attributable to a new predictor variable, here, showing whether and to what extent a higher therapeutic index showed a greater likelihood of success. The magnitude of effect, as indicated by the correlation coefficient r, was .92 ($r^2 = .85$) and was equivalent in practical magnitude to increasing the likelihood of treatment success rate from 4 percent to 96 percent.

After calculating the value of every therapist's statement in cases 1 and 2, the data points were entered into a statistical program. Statistical analyses were performed with the computer program FASTAT, developed by Mark Bjerknes, which calculates the mean of the series. The mean of the series is the mean therapeutic index for an individual therapist during one session. Transforming the data in this manner allowed us to compare mean therapeutic effectiveness and to plot the data.

The data were smoothed to remove the point-to-point wobbles and jumps that make it hard to see the general shape. The smoothing was done by using a running smoother. For instance, a three-point running smoother takes a three-unit "window" for each value of the series. It calculates the mean of the three values and then records that value as the "smoothed" value for that window. It then moves the window to the next data point and calculates the average, and so on until the end of the series. The smoothed series is then plotted as a graphic with the number of verbal statements represented on the X axis (time) and the value of the therapeutic index on the Y axis.

Discussion: Case Analysis
GRAPHIC DATA DISPLAY

The variability of the index across time can be shown by the graphic data display of the series. The methods and the forms of data analysis used in psychotherapy research have usually isolated practitioners from their clinical performance. In general, the procedures do not capture variations in therapeutic performance. The methods used in our project were designed to describe patterns in the therapeutic interaction that are not tapped by unidimensional variables. A way of further expanding the information gathered about the therapeutic interaction is by using graphic data display.

The graphical display attains particular importance as a comprehensive means of interpreting trends over time in a form that allows rapid assimilation and assessment by the reader. The analysis is essentially a visual process. The schematic data plotting is a useful way for "seeing what is going on" in therapy across time (Tukey, 1977). Changes in the ongoing therapeutic effectiveness of the therapist's actions are recorded, providing a visual "topographic" summary of the therapeutic interaction. This summary has clinical utility because it gives behavioral referents to the scale that may be useful for referring to the transcript of the session.

Figure 5.1a shows case 1, in which the mean therapeutic index is 2.86. It shows that the session begins at a positive index level. Also, figure 1a shows a pattern in which there are two sudden declines to a negative level: after statement 25 and statement 80. Changes in the index level represent intrasession variations that are not normally revealed by conventional statistical analysis. The changes in level during a session might be of applied importance because it is possible to return to the transcript and analyze the nature of the interaction at the point at which the index level decreased. For instance, the transcript revealed that the consultant (statements 12–40)

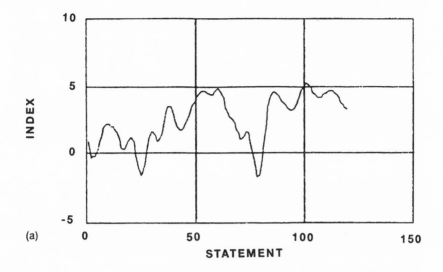

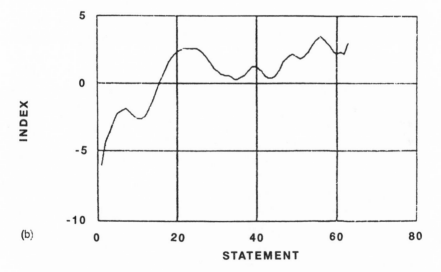

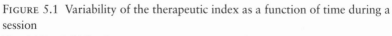

FIGURE 5.1 Variability of the therapeutic index as a function of time during a session

Note: (a) Case 1; (b) Case 2.

was asking family members where they were while the mother was at-tempting suicide (material, noninducers). Also, the transcript revealed that at statement 80 the topic of conversation shifted. The mother and the fa-ther suddenly began arguing about the father's drinking problem. The ther-apist interrupted, asking the father for information (material [0]) and stat-ing his opinion about alcoholism (noninducer [0]).

Figure 5.1b shows case 2, in which the mean index is .714. In compari-son to case 1 it shows that the session begins at a negative therapeutic index level and later reaches a positive level. Analysis of the transcript reveals that the consultant spent much time in the early part of the session collecting information (material, noninducers) about the mother's recent hysterec-tomy. Also, the figure shows fewer fluctuations than in case 1. Once a posi-tive index level is reached, it is maintained throughout the session.

The plotting of the index is a preliminary analysis of the observed vari-ability in a therapist's effectiveness across time. Here, the therapist is the unit of analysis, and it is therapeutic effectiveness on which our research interest focuses. So, to characterize effectiveness adequately, every therapist being studied was examined repeatedly over time, and a longitudinal "ef-fectiveness record" systematically was assembled for each therapist. Prelim-inary analyses of these observed effectiveness records were aided by calcu-lating the therapeutic mean and plotting and inspecting, for each therapist, the therapeutic effectiveness trajectories—simple graphs of the therapeutic index displayed against time (statement number).

Next, it is important to investigate whether therapeutic effectiveness seems to grow in the same fashion, with the same shape to its growth, and at the same rates or curvatures (Willett, Ayoub, and Robinson, 1991). Inspection of the within-in therapist effectiveness trajectories in this study suggested that despite the considerable scatter during the session, a straight-line-growth model provided a robust and convenient summary of changes in therapeutic effectiveness over time. The straight-line-growth model in this study represented therapeutic effectiveness, index, as a linear function of time, t, in statement number.

In this model, the intercept represents therapeutic effectiveness at time zero. In our example, case 1 had a positive intercept of .545 whereas case 2 had a negative intercept of –1.745. Thus, the data showed that the thera-pist in case 2 began the session with a negative index, suggesting that at the beginning of the session therapeutic effectiveness was negative and low compared to case 1, which was positive and moderately high. In this model, the slope represents the rate at which therapeutic effectiveness is changing during the session. In our example, case 1 has a slope of .033 and case 2 has a slope of .075. Thus, the data showed that in case 2 therapeutic effectiveness is increasing at almost twice the rate of that in case 1.

DISCUSSION

Here we have described a method for measuring therapeutic interactions and showed its application to different theoretical schools. The method operationally defines the practice of therapy as a therapist interacting with a patient with the goal of transforming the assessments of relations and dimensions embedded in a patient's discourse. There are of course different schools of therapy that provide different theoretical explanations of how to do this (Giacomo and Weissmark, 1986, 1987). But at the level of practice, as opposed to theory, the actions of the therapists are functionally equivalent.

At the level of practice, therapists do basically three things: they encourage patients to assess relationships or material attributes; they match or do not match the relationships appraised by patients; and they induce patients to shift their appraisals from external to internal, from reactive to selective, and from unconditional to conditional or they instruct (noninducer) patients. The mean therapeutic index quantifies the degree to which a therapist uses these operations to evoke changes. The results show that cases 1 and 2 had a moderately positive index, suggesting that expert therapists use the combined therapeutic operations—assessing relations, matching relations, and inducing.

The results are consistent with previous findings of a statistically significant and strongly positive relation between the therapeutic index and treatment outcome. The data showed that, on the average, therapists of a successful therapy encourage patients to assess relationships when describing their difficulties. They match the relationships appraised by the patients. And they induce changes in the patients' appraisal of the three dimensions—from external to internal, from reactive to selective, and from unconditional to conditional (Giacomo and Weissmark, 1992a, 1992b; Weissmark and Giacomo, 1994). The overall pattern of the previous findings suggested what a therapist does in therapy has an impact on outcome.

The plotting of the index against time allows for tracking the moment-to-moment changes in a therapist's effectiveness in establishing conditions to help patients change their assessments. The variability in the index across time is consistent with an emerging body of evidence suggesting the patient-therapist relationship does not usually follow a linear development throughout therapy but has a fluctuating course with a series of break-downs and repairs. Safran et al. (1990) have found, for example, that positive outcome was most closely associated with successful repairs and alliance ruptures. Similarly, Horvath and Marx (1991) have described the course of the alliance in successful therapy as a series of developments, decays, and repairs.

These results also extend the findings of studies relating treatment outcomes to various relationship factors. Most researchers, however, have sought simple associations between single relationship variables—for instance, the presence or absence of a specific therapist quality (whether a therapist is actively involved, empathetic, genuine or supportive)—and outcome. Researchers agree that what is needed now is a more complex multidimensional and context-sensitive approach to process research in which a profile of measures is used to describe behaviors across time.

The method described here was designed to take the context of the ongoing therapist-patient exchange and the sequential nature of the therapeutic process into account. The therapeutic index is an interactional, multidimensional measure of therapeutic effectiveness. It quantifies each therapeutic statement in relation to the patient statement that preceded it. Thus, it is in keeping with the recent call for more clinically relevant research that preserves the ecological validity of the therapeutic process.

The fallacy in studies that rate process on single variables in isolation from their context is that all therapist behaviors receiving the same rating on a single dimension (such as level of empathy or self-disclosure) are assumed to have the same therapeutic significance and the same effect on outcome. A therapist matching a relation that a patient is assessing and inducing the patient to assess it conditionally, after which the patient changes his or her appraisal of that relation from reactive to selective, is a far more accurate description of a therapeutic interaction than a single dimensional description such as empathic reflection. This degree of descriptive specificity greatly enhances our ability to depict in-therapy performance. And it is these multidimensional descriptions of the process that will enable reliable description of phenomena at a level of clinical relevance. Thus, terms such as *validation* and *empathy* may be understood to be a generic reference to the more specific therapeutic operation of reformulating a family member's discourse into matched relational terms.

From a practical perspective, the method described here has proven helpful for teaching clinical skills. One major issue in clinical training and evaluation is finding an efficient way of improving trainees' relationship skills by a structured process. To date there are no measures or criteria available that are precise enough to assess the many and varied ways of developing relationship skills. At first, it may seem that a single therapeutic index may reduce the training utility of the method. The possibility of referring from the graphic data display to the coding sheet, and from the coding sheet to the transcript, however, is still possible. This process of referring to the transcript has been proven useful in practice and in teaching. It can be used for assessing interactional sequences in the content of a therapist's speech in the peaks and valleys of the curve. This makes the method a valuable tool for training because it can be used for standardizing, reconstructing, and comparing trainees' relationship skills within and across sessions.

To conclude, let us point out some limitations of the method and suggest some improvements. Clinical experience suggests timing is an important determinant of treatment outcome. The coding method, however, does not consider the timing of therapeutic interventions. A therapist statement that matches the relationships assessed by a patient and induces changes in the patient's assessments of the three dimensions—from external to internal, from reactive to selective, and from unconditional to conditional—gets a high index despite the timing of that statement.

The plotting of the index is a preliminary analysis of the observed variability in a therapist's effectiveness. The method takes advantage of longitudinal data to estimate changes in therapeutic effectiveness over time (statements during a session). The accurate measurement of growth is crucial if change in therapeutic effectiveness is to be adequately detected and described. In our analyses, we have represented the empirical effectiveness trajectories by smooth and continuous functions of time. Thus, we have elected to represent the changes in therapeutic effectiveness by a linear growth model, and the adequacy of our analyses rests on this assumption. However, when therapeutic effectiveness is well measured, more complex and substantively appealing representations might be profitably used. Theories of therapeutic effectiveness may suggest, for instance, that nonlinear growth curves are more appropriate. Such refinements can easily be tested when multidimensional data are available and will add greatly to the quality of our analysis of therapeutic effectiveness. Although the standard adage that "more research is needed" certainly applies to every aspect of psychotherapy and psychotherapy training, we think that more research than ever will be needed before exciting tools exist for measuring therapeutic interactions.

Summing Up

The results of our work support the hypothesis that the therapeutic index is strongly predictive of treatment outcome. The study of specific patterns in therapeutic actions, as quantified by the mean therapeutic index early in treatment, differentiated between successful and unsuccessful cases. On the average, the verbal statements of therapists of a successful therapy yielded a higher index than those of an unsuccessful therapy.

The results also show the possibility of tracking the moment-to-moment variability of a single therapist's effectiveness. The graphic data display is a simple graph of index values displayed against time. Graphic data display can be used to represent trends of performance over time.

These results have theoretical and practical implications for the field of psychotherapy. Competing theories have defined psychotherapy in many ways. We think it is seems consistent with most theories to suggest it is a process of interpersonal persuasion in which the therapist influences the patient to assume responsibility. A major question that researchers continue to grapple with is, What specific therapist operations influence patients' progress?

Most researchers have sought simple associations between single therapist variables—such as the presence or absence of a specific therapist quality—and outcome. By contrast, the method described here was designed to take the context of the ongoing therapist-patient exchange and the sequential nature of the psychotherapeutic process into account. Thus, it is in keeping with the recent call for more clinically relevant research that preserves the ecological validity of psychotherapy process. As such, the method involves the detailed analysis of individual cases based on complete transcripts.

A therapeutic index measure can be obtained from the analysis. The therapeutic index is about the system of interactional links created by the patient and the therapist. The index is a transactional, multidimensional measure of therapeutic effectiveness. It quantifies each therapeutic statement in relation to the patient statement that preceded it. Research has shown that early in treatment patients' statements are, on the average, external, reactive, and unconditional. During treatment, therapists continuously assess the multidimensional patterns contained in patients' statements. Therapeutic interventions are directed toward producing shifts in the multidimensional patterns underlying patients' responses. Patients of a successful therapy are more likely to shift their assessments from external to internal, from reactive to selective, and from unconditional to conditional.

Therapeutic interventions aimed at producing shifts in the multidimensional patterns underlying patients' responses are seen as being multifaceted. Each facet of a therapist's action is measured by a therapist variable. This dimensional analysis of each therapeutic action allows for the structural analysis of the patient-therapist interaction. Within this framework, it is possible to classify therapists' actions along a continuum of therapeutic effectiveness. The different degrees of effectiveness are related to the types of dimensions assessed by a therapist.

At one extreme of this spectrum of effectiveness there is a high-interactive profile that is characterized by a therapist who induces a patient to assess relationships and shift assessments and is sensitive to the relationships assessed by a patient. At the other extreme of the continuum there is a low-interactive profile that is characterized by a therapist who instructs changes in a patient, does not induce a patient to assess relationships or shift assessments, and is not sensitive to the relationships assessed by the patient. The therapeutic index quantifies these patterns along a continuum. From a practical perspective, the therapeutic index has proven helpful for measuring therapeutic effectiveness and for improving clinical training.

6

Clinical Applications

If you want to find out anything from the theoretical physicists about the methods they use, I advise you to stick closely to one principle. Don't listen to their words, fix your attention on their deeds.

Albert Einstein

In previous chapters, we have emphasized the difference between theoretical knowledge and practical knowledge. Theoretical knowledge is based on logical thinking; practical knowledge is based on analogical thinking. When therapists use theoretical knowledge, they are using logical thinking to fit the specifics of a case to general principles. When therapists use practical knowledge, they are using analogical thinking to focus on the similarities among the specifics. They see, for instance, thematic patterns in the stories patients tell.

There is no contradiction between theoretical knowledge and practical knowledge. Doing therapy requires therapists to use both types of knowledge. Theoretical knowledge is useful for applying standard techniques, whereas practical knowledge is useful for dealing with the dynamics. As Minuchin and Fishman put it, "The therapist finds himself with two different sets of information. One is the dynamics of the human interaction. The other is the specific operation of the therapeutic encounter. It is as though he had a list of words on the one hand and an epic poem in the other" (1981, p. 5).

When therapists use theoretical knowledge, they are trying to mold the therapeutic encounter to fit their theories. "Theories," Luchins (1942) said, "are like a procrustean bed to which the situation must conform. . . ." (p. 93). Theories and the techniques derived from theories are useful for helping therapists focus on specific patients' behaviors, feelings, or thoughts. For example, the cognitive technique of eliciting automatic thoughts focuses therapists' attention on patients' thoughts, whereas the supportive-expressive technique of listening focuses therapists' attention on patients' feelings about relationships. Therapists use these standard techniques because it helps them shape the therapeutic encounter into a familiar, predictable situation. This in turn helps therapists draw general conclusions about how to solve patients' problems.

But patients do not belong to theoretical approaches. There are no cognitive, psychodynamic, or interpersonal patients. Patients are simply people. And therapists are people, too! Despite therapists' theoretical preferences, they still have to relate to patients as people. They have to apply techniques and theories to real human encounters, and in human encounters unexpected things may occur. Therapists may be faced with unique situations that fall outside the categories of applied theory. A situation may become something other than the one planned for; therefore, therapists have to use their practical knowledge, too.

In this chapter, we illustrate how therapists use their practical and theoretical knowledge in the work of everyday practice. We begin by describing a depressed patient. We then briefly review three theoretical approaches: the cognitive, the supportive-expressive, and the interpersonal. We then show how therapists (from each of these approaches) view the same patient. We also illustrate how therapists apply their theories and standard techniques to the practice situation. Finally, we focus on therapists' practical knowledge. We show that despite differences in theoretical approaches therapists use similar practical knowledge to manage the dynamic aspects of the therapeutic encounter.

A Case Example: Cognitive, Supportive-Expressive, and Interpersonal Approaches

The patient was a forty-year-old white female teacher whose main problem was depression. She came for treatment because she felt "sad all the time" and "useless." Her primary symptoms were depressed mood, low self-esteem, loss of appetite, and lack of interest. The patient reported, "My marital relationship is awful." She complained her husband was "holding me back" and "taking me for granted." The patient spoke about feeling helpless and angry because "my husband doesn't pay much attention to me." She said she felt "neglected" and "isolated." The patient described a lifelong inability to form intimate relationships with friends and relatives.

THE COGNITIVE APPROACH

The cognitive approach assumes that depression comes from distortions in a patient's interpretations of events. Beck maintains that a person's cognitive system intervenes between external impingements and behavioral responses. According to Beck, the cognitive system operates by thoughts and a matrix of *schemas*. Beck (1967) defines a *schema* as "a cognitive structure for screening, coding, and evaluating the stimuli that impinge on the organism. . . . On the basis of [these] schemas, the individual is able to orient himself in relation to time and space and to categorize and interpret experiences in a meaningful way" (p. 283).

Beck maintains that schemas are dynamic structures that change throughout a person's lifetime. Normally a person changes his or her schemas; if, however, the schemas are fixed, they become maladaptive. A maladaptive schema "refers to extremely stable and enduring themes that develop during childhood and are elaborated upon throughout the individual's lifetime. . . . For example, a child may develop the schema that no matter what he/she does, his/her performance will never be good enough. . . . Once the schema is activated, the [person] categorizes, selects, and encodes information in such a way that the failure schema is maintained" (Young, Beck, and Weinberger, 1993, p. 242). Fixed schemas make a person's cognitions maladaptive, which in turn can cause depressive thinking. Depressed patients distort their interpretations of events and maintain a negative view of themselves, their environment, and their future. Cognitive therapy focuses on changing patients' depressive thinking.

Using the case example described above, the following interview is an example of how a therapist uses cognitive techniques to change a patient's depressive thinking.

A Cognitive Interview

A cognitive therapist structures the interview logically. The therapist breaks down the patient's complaints into a specific set of problems that can be corrected. Then the therapist sets an agenda to tackle the problems in order of priority.

The Inductive Questioning Technique

After an agenda is set, the therapist begins by eliciting the patient's automatic thoughts. The following excerpt illustrates how a cognitive therapist uses inductive questioning to discover the patient's automatic thoughts.

T: Now, try to remember the time when you last felt depressed.
P: It was yesterday. I was at home alone and I started feeling very sad, I don't even know why . . .

T: What kind of thoughts did you say you were having?

P: Well, they were all kinds of thoughts. Mostly, being angry with my husband, Bob, you know, the kind of life I have . . . feeling sad all the time and dealing with the fact that he's never home.

T: What happened?

P: I was thinking about what I could do . . . like for a long time I've been considering joining something, like a dance class or something, and I haven't been able to do it. My husband doesn't like when I do things by myself.

T: Is that why you haven't pursued your own interests?

P: I'm just not good at doing anything. That's why people don't like being with me.

In this exchange, the therapist has discovered the patient's automatic thought, "People avoid me because I'm not good enough."

The Examining-Evidence Technique

According to Young and Beck (1982), "Once the therapist and patient have identified a key automatic thought, the therapist may ask the patient . . . to view the thought as a hypothesis to be tested" (p. 196). There are several techniques to modify automatic thoughts. One is the examining-evidence technique. The following excerpt illustrates how a cognitive therapist uses the examining-evidence technique.

T: OK, so you think your husband spends time working because you aren't good enough for him.

P: Yeah.

T: Why do you think that?

P: Otherwise he would be spending more time with me.

T: Do you think anyone close to you appreciates you?

P: Yes, my father did, before he died . . .

T: Was he always with you?

P: Ah, no, but when he was he really appreciated me.

T: Maybe, we can work on you getting your husband's appreciation when you are together.

In this exchange, the therapist has helped the patient examine the available evidence and identified logical contradictions.

The Identifying-Assumptions Technique

Young and Beck (1982) maintain that cognitive therapists "often observe general patterns that seem to underlie patients' automatic thoughts. These patterns or regularities act as a set of rules that guide the way a patient reacts to many different situations. We refer to these rules as 'assumptions.' . . . One of the major goals of cognitive therapy is to help patients identify and challenge those maladaptive assumptions. . . . In order to identify these maladaptive assumptions, the therapist can listen closely for themes that seem to cut across several different situations or problem areas. The therapist can then list several related automatic thoughts that the patient has already expressed on different occasions, and ask the patient to abstract the general rule that connects the automatic thoughts" (p. 200). According to Young and Beck, when these general rules are framed in absolute terms they often lead to disturbances such as depression. Automatic thoughts that lead to depression (or any other kind of faulty thinking) are called "maladaptive."

The following excerpt illustrates how a cognitive therapist tries to identify the main assumption of the patient's automatic thoughts.

> T: For instance, when you say your husband doesn't pay attention to you because he's always working, it sounds as though you're bothered because he spends time away from you.
> P: Yeah, I think he doesn't care about me or maybe he's found something better to do than spending time with me. Sometimes I even think he wants to leave me.
> T: So, one thing that really makes you feel bad is this idea that people you care about may leave you. Is that right?
> P: Yeah, and I get very depressed . . .
> T: Is there anything you can do about that?
> P: I have to make myself aware of the fact that sometimes my husband needs to stay away for a few days, for business reasons. That doesn't mean he's gonna abandon me. And the same with my mother . . .

In this exchange, the therapist has identified the main assumption of the patient's automatic thoughts: "People who care about me will leave me."

The Questioning-the-Validity-of-Assumptions Technique

The following excerpt illustrates how a cognitive therapist uses the questioning-the-validity-of-assumptions technique to encourage the patient to examine the effects of holding onto the automatic thought, "People who care about me will leave me."

T: I get the sense that you're always thinking you have to please your husband.

P: Well, you know, I think my husband believes married women shouldn't go out alone . . . you know, like if I would go to a club or something like that, he would be upset.

T: So, what do you think would happen if you started doing things independently?

P: Oh, I think he would get upset . . .

T: . . . And then what do you predict he would do? What would happen?

P: He might leave me . . . I guess. Then I think, "He works so hard and I'm just enjoying myself." I'd feel guilty about being selfish. So I stay at home. I feel if I don't please him he's gonna get fed up with me; so I end up doing nothing.

T: What about the other side of it? Are there any positive things you'd be giving up if he would be with you all the time?

P: Hmm, I never thought about that.

T: What about having personal time, perhaps going to aerobic classes like you mentioned? Would that be important to you at all?

COGNITIVE EXPLANATIONS

Cognitive theory assumes that depression comes from cognitive distortions. In the above example, we saw the therapist elicited the patient's distorted automatic thought "My husband avoids me because I'm not good enough for him." Then the therapist got the patient to test the validity of her distorted thought by having her examine the evidence. Specifically, the therapist encouraged the patient to question the belief "If my husband appreciated me he would spend more time with me." To do this, the therapist encouraged the patient to examine contradictory evidence such as "Your father appreciated you, but was he always with you?"

In the above example, we also saw that the therapist got the patient to identify the automatic, or maladaptive, assumption "People who care about me will leave me." To identify the assumption, the therapist listened for themes that cut across the patient's statements and identified the theme "People who are close to me will leave me." This theme or schema appeared in several of the patient's statements concerning her husband, mother, brother, and friends.

After the patient identified the maladaptive theme, the therapist got the patient to question its validity by exploring the consequences of holding on to the belief "People who care about me will leave me." More specifically, the therapist got the patient to consider the consequences of holding on to the belief "One should be close to loved ones, even if it means sacrificing one's own interests and needs." The therapist asked the patient, "Are there any positive things you'd be giving up if he would be with you all the time?"

In brief, cognitive theory assumes that maladaptive belief systems lead to depression and self-defeating behaviors. Therapy involves training in the correction of faulty thinking so that maladaptive thoughts are replaced with adaptive ones. The standard therapeutic techniques of inductive questioning, examining evidence, identifying assumptions, and questioning the validity of assumptions focus on the development of new adaptive thoughts.

THE SUPPORTIVE-EXPRESSIVE APPROACH

Supportive-expressive (psychodynamic) theory assumes that depression comes from intrapsychic conflicts. Luborsky (1984) maintains that a person's personality system integrates psychological, biological, and cultural experiences through "psychological representations." The psychological representations are expressed as wishes, intentions, or needs. Murray (1938) defines a "need" as a cognitive affective concept that organizes behavior "in such a way as to transform in a certain direction an existing, unsatisfying situation" (pp. 123–24).

Other psychodynamic authors describe psychological representations as dynamic structures that change according to an individual's maturational processes (Rosenblatt and Thikstun, 1977). These authors have claimed that normally individuals adapt to developmental and environmental changes by producing changes in their psychological representations; however, sometimes a person's psychological representations become fixed and inconsistent. An important developmental task is to integrate the inconsistencies.

Inconsistencies among the fixed psychological representations may result in conflicts. *Conflicts,* according to the psychodynamic view, refers to fixed psychological representations that develop during childhood and are maintained throughout the life span. For example, a woman may have the wish "to be open and honest in all relationships." But if, in the past, she avoided family conflicts by "keeping quiet," then she might have difficulty in other intimate relationships. The inconsistency between "being open" and "keeping quiet" may produce a psychological conflict.

According to Luborsky (1984), conflicts form a "core conflictual relationship theme." These themes are relationship patterns "ready to be actualized in relationship after relationship, like a theme and variations on a theme . . . in spite of their self-hurtful nature" (pp. 17–18). Symptoms, including depression, can result from conflictual relationship patterns. Supportive-expressive therapy focuses on helping people understand their conflictual relationship patterns.

Using the case described above, the following interview is an example of how a therapist uses standard supportive-expressive techniques to help the patient gain insight into her conflictual relationship patterns.

A SUPPORTIVE-EXPRESSIVE INTERVIEW

Supportive-expressive therapists are instructed to structure their sessions in a logical fashion. Luborsky (1984) points out that therapists "listen in order to establish what the patient's problems are and let the patient try to cast these in terms of goals ordered in importance" (p. 61). According to Luborsky, the goals also make clear the ends to be achieved and help therapist and patient monitor progress in relation to initial goals. After the goals are set, Luborsky says, the therapist's basic task is to listen and evaluate what the patient is communicating. "The therapist sets the stage for the patient to express through thoughts and feelings and to listen and reflect on them with the aim of understanding" and changing what needs to be changed (p. 90).

According to Luborsky, the therapist's main goal is to understand the central relationship problems related to the patient's symptoms. "The understanding is about some facets of the current relationship problems and those aspects of the past ones that may have contributed to them" (p. 23).

The Listening Technique

The following excerpt illustrates how a supportive-expressive therapist uses the listening technique to identify the central relational episode.

    T: When did you visit your mother?

    P: Last Saturday. I was trying to enjoy my day off, but then, I don't know, I found myself going to my mother's.

    T: So, did you drive there?

    P: Well, I was downtown and I thought, "I'm near my mother's house, maybe I should visit her." I wanted to ask her about the problems I've been having with my husband, Bob. But she didn't want to get involved. She's always been like that.

    T: So, then what happened?

    P: Well, I didn't know what to do. When she reacts like that I can't decide on my own. Because when I try and make decisions she tells me I should have done something else.

    T: Is that what paralyzes you?

    P: Yeah, when she withdraws like that I just start feeling really bad.

In this exchange, the therapist has identified the central relational episode expressed as the patient's wish, "I wish to be close to my mother."

The Understanding Technique

The following excerpt illustrates how the therapist uses the understanding technique to identify the same relation in other episodes.

    T: So, you feel your brother never felt comfortable with your friends. He had his own separate life . . .

    P: Right, I think so.

    T: You think so?

    P: Pretty much; he's always been aloof.

    T: Is anyone in the family close to you?

    P: No. I'm not really close to anyone.

    T: Why aren't you close to anyone in the family? Did anything happen that has prevented you from feeling close to them?

    P: Yeah, they tried to force me to stay at home.

    T: Do you feel you might get close again sometime, on your own terms?

According to Luborsky (1984), "When more than one [relationship] instance . . . is available from the same patient, the principle of redundancy across contexts can contribute to understanding. Inspecting the contexts in sequence allows recognition of significant redundancies in the components of relationship themes. . . . After each episode is identified, some inferences will be drawn about the relational theme; at the end, a clinical formulation of the main relationship conflict is given based on all the examples together" (p. 101). Luborsky maintains that identifying the relationship theme is based on finding the pattern of the patient's relationships with others.

In the above exchange, the therapist identified the patient's main relationship conflict expressed as the wish "I wish to be close to them. But I fear they are going to control me."

The Responding-to-the-Core-Theme Technique

After understanding the core relational theme, the therapist responds. The response, Luborsky says, should address the core theme and its associated symptoms. The following excerpt illustrates how the therapist responds to the core theme.

T: Has the relationship with your mother always been the way you just described it? You get depressed when she is aloof?

P: Yeah, she's always been that way with everyone.

T: How does her lack of involvement affect your mood?

P: I get depressed about it.

T: Have you been able to discuss with her how you feel about not being close to her?

P: I feel that I can stop myself from getting upset. I respect her ways as long as she respects my ways and as long as she doesn't try to control me.

The Working-Through Technique

According to Luborsky (1984), a patient's improvement depends on his or her ability to master relational problems. Improvement depends on how much the patient can work through his or her conflicts. The therapist's task is to engage the patient in a working-through of edition after edition of the relationship problems as they are expressed in the relationship with the therapist. This process, Luborsky writes, facilitates the patient's change in the course of the therapy by offering opportunities to re-experience the relationship problems as they appear with the therapist, that is, in the transference. By the end of treatment, "the patient tends to find more adaptive ways of behaving, even though the elements of the early relationship patterns tend to be still discernible" (p. 23).

The following excerpt illustrates how a supportive-expressive therapist helps the patient work through her conflict.

T: Do you feel that I'm always in charge here?
P: Oh, I know you are the professional.
T: Even if that's so here, what about outside therapy in your everyday life, are you in charge?
P: No, I don't feel that way.
T: Who is in charge then?
P: I'm not sure. Things have been going so well lately. I decided about the vacations and then several other things came up and I handled myself well. But last week I felt scared. After you said I didn't need to come to therapy so frequently, I realized I don't feel ready for other kinds of decisions.
T: Well, sooner or later, you'll need to decide based on what you've accomplished here whether you still need me around.
P: I know.
T: Or whether, as long as you are all right, you want to continue on your own.

PSYCHODYNAMIC EXPLANATIONS

Psychodynamic theory assumes that depression results from conflicts. In the above example, we saw that the therapist identified the core conflictual relational episode. The therapist got the patient to describe two relational episodes, one with her mother and the other with her brother. In both episodes, the patient expressed the same wish to be close to her family.

In the above example, we also saw how the therapist used the relational episodes to understand the core—"I wish to be close"—and the consequences—"But I am fearful I'll be dominated"—of that wish. The therapist then encouraged the patient to see how the core conflictual relational theme related to her depressive symptoms.

After the patient understood how the relational theme related to her symptoms, the therapist got the patient to work through her conflict. Part of working through the conflict involved experiencing and enacting the issue of control in the therapeutic relationship. The therapist asked the patient, "Do you feel that I'm always in charge here?" "Sooner or later, you'll need to decide based on what you've accomplished here whether you still need me around."

In brief, psychodynamic theory assumes that core conflictual relational patterns can lead to depression. Therapy involves helping patients to gain insight into the roots of their conflictual relational patterns so that they can find more adaptive ways of behaving. The reenactment of these conflictual patterns in relation to the therapist provides the basis for insight. The standard therapeutic techniques of listening, understanding, responding, and working through focus on helping patients achieve insight into their conflictual relational patterns.

The Interpersonal Approach

Interpersonal theory assumes that depression comes from a disruption in personal bonds. According to Sullivan (1940), "A personality can never be isolated from the complex of interpersonal relations in which the person lives and has his being . . . personality is made manifest in interpersonal situations, and not otherwise" (p. 32).

Borrowing from Sullivan, Klerman et al. (1984) maintain that an individual's behavior occurs in a psychosocial, interpersonal context. The interpersonal self involves knowledge and emotion shaped by the individual's roles and social position. "Each person holds multiple hierarchical positions in the social system and play specific roles appropriate to these positions" (p. 48). Other authors define "roles" as dispositional schemas involving affective, cognitive, or sensorimotor representations and processes that elaborate one's identity and guide one's behavior between self and others (Wiley and Alexander, 1987).

According to Klerman et al. (1984), roles and interpersonal relationships change throughout the life span. Disruption in interpersonal relationships during the course of development—by death, loss, or separation—may influence the way people establish new relationships. Over time, people develop patterns of maladaptive interpersonal relatedness. These patterns are stable and fixed relational patterns that develop during childhood and are elaborated on throughout an individual's lifetime. A fixed relational pattern may interfere with a person's ability to adapt to stress and changes. This, in turn, may lead to weaker social bonds, fewer attachments, and less social support. The lack of intimacy, social integration, and strong social bonds may lead to depressive symptoms. The focus of interpersonal therapy is to assist patients to master their social roles and to modify their interpersonal relationships.

Using the case described above, the interview below is an example of how a therapist uses interpersonal techniques to help the patient modify her interpersonal relationships.

An Interpersonal Interview

The interpersonal therapist works to "help patients identify their problems, make choices about a plan of action, and modify the maladaptive patterns for a satisfactory resolution of the symptoms" (Klerman et al., 1984, p. 91). Therapists are instructed to identify the problem area and to set up a treatment contract. "It is important to define the problem areas because they can help the . . . therapist outline realistic goals and follow appropriate treatment strategies" (p. 91). After the agenda is set, the therapist elicits the patient's view of his or her interpersonal relationships.

The Nondirective Exploratory Technique

The following excerpt illustrates how the therapist explores the interpersonal role dispute between the patient and her husband.

T: And how do you feel about your husband?
P: I feel that despite my efforts, he's become a different person.
T: What do you mean by "different"?
P: He's become very "cold." We never spend time discussing anything. He doesn't share my values. We are like strangers under the same roof, not even that, 'cause he's always away on business trips.
T: Is there anything else that is different?
P: Yeah, he also interferes with my confidence to make decisions; he thinks I always should consult with him.
T: Is that what makes you so unhappy?
P: Yeah! I end up stuck here at home and he's always gone.

In this exchange, the therapist has helped the patient see the issues involved in the role dispute with her husband.

The Clarification Technique

The following excerpt illustrates how the therapist uses the clarification technique to help the patient understand the difference between her expectations and her husband's expectations.

T: So you feel your husband got you into this situation. Do you have a sense of how he sees his being away, and his involvement in the business?

P: No, not really.

T: Well, what do you think?

P: He'd say he's never with me because he's busy establishing the business. He's always saying that it has nothing to do with me.

T: Was he close to you before he started the business?

P: Yes. He was a lot more involved before he opened the business.

T: Is there anything besides the business that keeps him away from you?

P: Yeah, he thinks that even if we spend more time together that wouldn't change the way I feel about the marriage.

T: Is it possible for you to try new ways of getting closer to him? Perhaps in ways that he wouldn't experience as interfering with the business?

In this exchange, the therapist has helped the patient understand how differences in her expectations and her husband's expectations are related to the role dispute.

The Communication-Analysis Technique

The following excerpt illustrates how the therapist helps the patient find a resolution to the role dispute. The therapist changes the focus of treatment from exploration and understanding to making decisions and taking action. The excerpt shows how the therapist uses the communication-analysis technique to help the patient become aware of how she communicates with her husband. The interpersonal approach maintains that awareness can lead to communicational changes in a person's maladaptive patterns.

T: So do you think you've clearly told your husband how you feel about his lack of involvement in the marriage?

P: Probably not in those terms. But after all these years just about anyone could figure out how upset I get when he is uninvolved.

T: Right, but you've said before that when he is uninvolved you really can't do anything about it because you think he may just get fed up and leave.

P: Right, and I get sad about it, too.

T: On the other hand, when he felt you were uninvolved and sort of

> pushing him away, you could communicate the issue very clearly to
> him, and I don't remember you saying he got upset.
> P: Well, but he was sick then and I remember making a conscious ef-
> fort to control myself while he was sick.

In this exchange, the therapist has helped the patient see that she expects
her husband to recognize her needs though she does not clearly communicate her needs to him.

The Directive Technique

The following excerpt illustrates how the therapist uses directive techniques
to help the patient evaluate her options.

> T: Why do you always let him decide for you?
> P: He gets very angry if I disregard what he says . . .
> T: What about when you decide about your personal things?
> P: It doesn't matter to him.
> T: He still gets angry?
> P: Mm-hmm, I guess my options are to start having my own life, or
> to make my own decisions and forget about him, or to get sepa-
> rated.
> T: What about if your husband would accept your needs and would
> understand that you don't want to sacrifice yourself to save the mar-
> riage?
> P: I've got to be convinced of that first!
> T: You wouldn't give up your freedom even if he promised you every-
> thing would be OK?

In this exchange, the therapist has helped the patient analyze the situation
and choose among options.

INTERPERSONAL EXPLANATIONS

Interpersonal theory assumes that depression results from a disruption in
interpersonal bonds. In the above example, we saw how the therapist got
the patient to explore her relationship with her husband: "We never spend
time discussing anything. He doesn't share my values. We are like strangers
under the same roof, not even that, 'cause he's always away on business
trips."

We also saw how the therapist got the patient to clarify the differences between her expectations and her husband's expectations. Then the therapist encouraged the patient to consider ways of being close to him that would meet his expectations, too. "Is it possible for you to try new ways of getting closer to him? Perhaps in ways that he wouldn't experience as interfering with the business?"

In the above example, we also saw that the therapist got the patient to identify her maladaptive communicational patterns. The therapist helped her to see the importance of communicating clearly: "When he felt you were uninvolved and sort of pushing him away, you could communicate the issue very clearly to him."

After getting the patient to understand her communicational patterns, the therapist tried to find a resolution to the dispute by getting the patient to evaluate her options. "I guess my options are to start having my own life, or to make my own decisions and forget about him, or to get separated."

In brief, interpersonal theory assumes that disruptions in interpersonal relations can lead to depression. Therapy involves guiding the patient through reviewing interpersonal issues most central to the patient's current depression. As the therapist guides the patient through the review, the goal is to get the patient to identify the dispute, then make choices about a plan of action, and finally modify maladaptive communication patterns or reassess expectations, for a satisfactory resolution of interpersonal disputes. The standard therapeutic techniques of exploration, clarification, communication analysis, and the directive technique focus on helping patients resolve their interpersonal disputes.

Case Review
LOGICAL ANALYSIS

Thus far in our discussion, we have sought to present three major theoretical approaches: the cognitive, the supportive-expressive, and the interpersonal. The first, the cognitive approach, postulates that depression results from distortions in a patient's interpretations of events. Accordingly, standard cognitive techniques focus on helping patients change their distorted cognitions. The second, the supportive-expressive approach, postulates that depression results from intrapsychic conflicts. Accordingly, standard supportive-expressive techniques focus on helping patients achieve insight into their conflictual relational patterns. The third, the interpersonal approach, places great stress on the disruption of personal bonds. Accordingly, standard interpersonal techniques focus on helping patients resolve their interpersonal disputes.

Although they differ in techniques and explanatory ideas, *all three approaches are similarly based on the logical mode of thought.* Applied to the clinical arena, the logical mode of thought assumes that therapists can define patients' problems, set goals for treatment, and follow a predetermined course of action. Furthermore, patients' problems are assumed to have a single cause that can be represented by a single dimension. Whether patients' problems are represented as disruptions in personal bonds, conflictual relational patterns, or distorted cognitions, all three approaches assume patients' problems are understandable, predictable, and solvable.

In the above examples, we showed how each therapist used standard techniques to understand and locate the patient's problem (represented as a single dimension). The cognitive therapist used the inductive questioning technique to find the maladaptive thought; the supportive-expressive therapist used the listening technique to find the conflictual relational episode; the interpersonal therapist used the nondirective exploratory technique to find the interpersonal dispute.

After locating patients' problems, the logical mode assumes therapists can apply their standard techniques to solve the problems. For instance, the cognitive approach assumes therapists can use cognitive techniques to change patients' maladaptive thoughts so their depression will decrease. In the above example, we showed how the cognitive therapist used the standard technique of questioning the validity of assumptions to change the patient's maladaptive thought.

The supportive-expressive approach assumes therapists can use supportive-expressive techniques to help patients understand their conflictual relational patterns so their depression will decrease. In the above example, we showed how the supportive-expressive therapist used the standard technique of working through to help the patient understand her conflict.

And the interpersonal approach assumes therapists can use interpersonal techniques to resolve patients' interpersonal disputes so their depression will decrease. In the above example, we showed how the interpersonal therapist used the standard technique of communication analysis to help the patient resolve her dispute.

Generally speaking, the logical mode assumes therapists are objective, rational decision makers who can categorize factual information about patients' problems, represent patients' problems in a single dimension, and apply theories and techniques to solve patients' problems. When these assumptions are stated explicitly, it becomes obvious that the logical mode cannot always be applied in the real world of practice. Although conceptually the logical mode is a beautiful thing, in the real world its usefulness is limited. In typical therapeutic situations, therapists, no matter how badly they want to do so, simply cannot follow theoretical procedures in a rigid, predetermined way. If doubt remains on this point, it can be dispelled by introspecting a bit about how therapists actually make therapeutic decisions.

ANALOGICAL ANALYSIS

In the real world of practice, most therapists are aware there is much uncertainty. The practice situation is uncertain because the very act of intervening may produce unexpected results. Therapists are unable to predict the consequences of their therapeutic actions, for example, the exact effect of using techniques on patients. The practice situation, having a life of its own, is distinct from therapists' intentions and may foil their technical moves. Situations of clinical practice are characterized by events that cannot be predicted before treatment takes place.

For these reasons, therapists have to rely on their practical knowledge, too. This kind of knowledge is essential; yet it often consists only of a vague intuitive feeling that certain things are relevant and others are not. This feeling is probably an outcome of previous experience that has not yet emerged into articulate thought. Sometimes, for instance, therapists suddenly have an "Aha!" experience. There is no doubt of the genuineness of the experience. It is an observable fact that therapists sometimes have an understanding of patients' situations suddenly. Moreover, the understanding therapists reach when they have these experiences, when they make sudden intuitive judgments, frequently are correct.

The explanation for therapists' sound intuitions is well known to researchers. It is no deeper than the explanation of our ability in a matter of seconds to recognize one of our friends among millions. We can do this not only with faces; we can do it in any field of expertise. Our ability to *recognize patterns* as old, familiar ones is what intuitive, practical knowledge is all about.

Practical knowledge, we have argued, is based on our ability to suddenly see the unfamiliar as familiar: to think analogically. Applied to the clinical arena, the analogical mode of thought assumes that therapists are subjective decision makers guided by the here and now of the practice situation. It assumes therapists must interpret patients' unpredictable behaviors. Furthermore, it assumes that therapists must deal with situations that are characterized by qualitative patterns that cannot be known before treatment takes place. To deal with unpredictable situations, therapists must depend on their practical knowledge—on their abilities to recognize relevant qualitative patterns.

In previous chapters, we defined these patterns as assessments of relations and dimensions. We said that patients used relations and dimensions to assess and organize their experiences. We operationally defined psychotherapy as a process in which therapists induce patients to shift their assessments from external to internal, from reactive to selective, and from unconditional to conditional. The therapeutic index measures how well therapists accomplish this task. It measures each therapist statement in relation to the patient statement that preceded it.

Assessing Relations

Returning to the case described above, we can see that all three therapists recognized the patient's pattern of relational assessments. That is to say, they recognized the pattern embedded in the patient's statements.

For instance, in the cognitive example the patient told the therapists she was angry at her husband for not being at home, "mostly, being angry at my husband, Bob . . . feeling sad all the time and dealing with the fact that he's never home." In a later exchange, the therapist said to the patient, "So, one thing that really makes you feel bad is this idea that people you care about may leave you." Here we can see that the therapist has recognized the patient's implicit relational assessment. It is reasonable to assume the patient does not literally mean her husband is "never at home." Rather, the therapist intuitively recognized that the patient's statement was a metaphorical way of assessing the relation "distance." The surface language of the statement does not contain the word *distance*, although distance is the relevant relation that underlined the patient's statements. When the therapist made sense of the patient's statements, he recognized the relevant relational pattern. The relevant relation, in this sense, is the relation that accounts for the centrally important features of the patient's statements—

that makes it understandable that certain elements of the situation are included in the statement while others are omitted.

In the supportive-expressive example the therapist also recognized the patient's relevant relational pattern. The patient told the therapist, "I wanted to ask her [mother] about the problems I've been having with my husband, Bob. But she didn't want to get involved." In a later exchange the therapist said, "Has the relationship with your mother always been the way you just described it? You get depressed when she is aloof?" Here we can see that the therapist recognized that the patient assessed the relation "distance" negatively. The therapist used the word *aloof* to account for the centrally important features of the patient's statements.

And finally, in the interpersonal example, the therapist also recognized the patient's negative assessment of distance. The patient told the therapist, "He's become very cold. We never spend time discussing anything. . . . We are like strangers under the same roof, not even that." In a later exchange the therapist said, "Do you have a sense of how he sees his being away?" Here we can see the therapist recognized that "He's become cold" and "being away" are both negative assessments of distance.

Thus, in all three examples we can see that the therapist has recognized the relevant relational assessments embedded in the patient's statements. The knowledge of what is relevant comes from accumulated experience— from a therapist's practical knowledge. Through analogical reasoning the therapist interprets the meaning of the patient's statement. Usually this is done intuitively. Probably, the therapist is unaware of what his brain actually does; he cannot recall many steps that actually must have been taken. If asked, most therapists would probably explain their actions in theoretical terms. These are the therapists' logical explanations of what they do (their theoretical approaches). However, the point we have been trying to make is that despite therapists' different theoretical explanations, at the level of practice therapists' actions are similar. In practice, therapists use analogical reasoning to recognize relational and dimensional patterns in patients' statements. Thus far in our discussion, we have illustrated how therapists recognize relational patterns. Now we will illustrate how therapists recognize dimensional patterns.

Assessing Dimensions

As we said before, therapists also recognize dimensional patterns in patients' relational assessments. And they induce patients to shift their assessments along three dimensions: from external to internal, from reactive to selective, and from unconditional to conditional. Returning to the case described above, we can see that all three therapists induced the patient to shift her assessments along the three dimensions.

For instance, in the cognitive example the therapist asked the patient, "So, what do you think would happen if you started doing things independently?" Here we can see that the therapist recognized the relation "autonomy." In a later exchange the patient said, "He might leave me . . . so I end up not doing anything." This statement shows that the patient evaluated the relation "closeness" unconditionally positive (she gives up doing things on her own to stay with her husband). Also, the statement shows the assessment was external (he might leave) and reactive (she doesn't have a choice in the matter). In a later exchange the patient said, "I'd feel guilty about being selfish . . . so I end up not doing anything." This statement shows that the patient evaluated the relation "autonomy" negatively ("I feel selfish"). Then the therapist asked the patient, "What about the other side of it? Are there any positive things you would be giving up if he would be with you all the time?" Here we can see that the therapist has recognized the relation "closeness" and has induced the patient to shift her assessment from unconditional (being close to her husband even if it means giving up doing things on her own) to conditional (the positive aspects of spending time alone); from external (he might leave) to internal (it depends on her decision); and from reactive (she has no choice because he might leave) to selective (she must decide whether to be with him).

In the supportive-expressive example the therapist recognized the dimensional patterns in the patient's statements. The therapist asked the patient, "Even if that's so here, what about outside of therapy in your everyday life, are you in charge?" Here we can see the therapist recognized the relation "autonomy." Later the patient replied, "After you said I didn't need to come to therapy so frequently, I realized I don't feel ready for other kinds of decisions." This statement shows the patient assessed the relation "autonomy" negatively ("I don't feel ready for other decisions"). The statement also shows that the assessment was external (the therapist told) and reactive (she can't make decisions). The therapist replied, "Well, sooner or later you'll need to decide, based on what you've accomplished here, whether you'll still need me around." Here we can see that the therapist has recognized the relation "autonomy" and has induced the patient to shift her assessment from unconditional ("I'm not ready to make decisions") to conditional ("based on what you've accomplished"); from external (the therapist told her) to internal (she will have to decide); and from reactive (she can't make decisions) to selective (it will be her choice).

And finally, in the interpersonal example the therapist also recognized the dimensional patterns in the patient's statements. The patient said, "He gets very angry if I disregard what he says." Here we can see the patient's assessment was external (he gets angry), reactive (there is nothing she can do about it), and unconditional (he always gets angry if she disregards what he says). The therapist replied, "What about when you decide about your personal things?" Here we can see that the therapist recognized the relation "autonomy" and induced the patient to shift her assessment from unconditional ("If I disregard what he says he gets angry") to conditional ("What about decisions regarding your personal things?"); from external (he gets angry) to internal ("Do you decide . . . ?"); and from reactive ("I can't disregard him") to selective ("Do you choose to decide about your personal things?").

Thus, in all three examples we can see that the therapist has recognized the relevant relational and dimensional patterns embedded in the patient's statements. The therapeutic index, which we described in chapter 5, measures how well the therapist does this. It codes the therapist's statement in relation to the patient statement that preceded it. For example, the following statements were coded:

Cognitive Interview

P: Well, you know, I think my husband believes married women shouldn't go out alone . . . you know, like if I would go to a club or something like that, he would be upset.

T: So, what do you think would happen if you started doing things independently?

Supportive-Expressive Interview

P: Oh, I know you are the professional.

T: Even if that's so here, what about outside of therapy in your everyday life? Are you in charge?

Interpersonal Interview

P: He gets very angry if I disregard what he says.

T: What about when you decide about your personal things?

In this example, the patient statements in all three interviews were coded as external (0), reactive (0), and unconditional (0), negative assessments of the relation "autonomy." The therapist statements, in all three interviews, were coded as internal (1), selective (1), conditional (1) assessments of the relation "autonomy." The therapeutic index was 8. (The index was calculated by using the weight system described in chapter 5.)

These examples show that whether patients' statements are generated by the questioning assumptions technique, the working-through technique, or the directive technique, the underlying structure is identical. Patients' statements (and therapists' statements, too) are expressions of relational and dimensional assessments. Because people use language to express their assessments the surface structure may differ, but beneath the surface there lies a similar structure.

Summing Up

Theoretical knowledge and practical knowledge are both important for doing psychotherapy. Theoretical knowledge is useful for defining patients' problems and applying standard techniques. However, in everyday practice therapists must apply their techniques in a real human encounter. This means that therapists must be prepared to deal with the dynamic aspects of practice. So therapists have to rely on their practical knowledge, too. Practical knowledge is useful for dealing with the uncertain, unique qualities of practice.

Although theoretical knowledge is well understood, practical knowledge remains vague. The difficulty is that knowledge that arises from practice has, to date, remained unspecifiable. The process by which the therapist arrives at a clinical decision still remains vague. Some of it is so vague that it has been called "intuition." Frequently, therapists cannot say with confidence exactly how they arrived at a clinical decision. They cannot point at the datum or the pattern of data that led to their decision. If asked, most therapists would explain their actions in theoretical terms. When two therapists are involved, one theoretical explanation is left to stand against another.

In brief, therapists' practical knowledge depends on a process they cannot trace. Since the clinical decision is the final standard, the ultimate measuring device against which other techniques are evaluated, and since this decision process is a vague one, it is hardly surprising that there is some question about whether scientific understanding is increasing in the field of psychotherapy.

So, to advance our understanding of the decision-making process in psychotherapy, we have sought to produce a retraceable process. That is to say, we have sought to define the process by which therapists make intuitive judgments. Such judgments, we have argued, depend on therapists' abilities to recognize patterns in patients' relational and dimensional assessments. These relations and dimensions are the basis for how patients organize their experiences. When people seek psychotherapy, it is often because they have organized their relational experiences in an unconditional, reactive, and external way. Whether it is termed a "maladaptive thought," "a core conflictual relation," or "an interpersonal dispute," the point we have tried to make is that the therapist has identified an underlying similarity in patients' relational and dimensional assessments.

Some authors have argued that the proliferation of terms and approaches in the field of psychotherapy has led to confusion. Yet it seems to us this is only natural in the development of a field. If, for example, we look at the history of numbers, the oldest records show that for centuries there were many different kinds of numerical systems: the hieroglyphics of the Egyptians, the queer figures of the Chinese, the cuneiform numerals of the Babylonians, the Roman numerals, and finally the Arabic numerals. Each system uses very different symbols. Yet despite their profound differences, they all refer to one mathematical reality.

Nevertheless, it took people centuries to accept the superiority of positional numeration, that is, the Arabic numerals. "Today, when positional numeration has become a part of our daily life, it seems that the superiority of this method . . . should have assured the rapid and sweeping acceptance of it. In reality, the transition, far from being immediate, extended over long centuries. In some places, Arabic numerals were banned from official documents; in others, the art was prohibited altogether" (Dantzig, 1954, p. 33).

Compared to the centuries that it took for people to accept Arabic numerals, it is understandable that psychotherapy is still in the stage of promoting different approaches. Still, we think, as mentioned in the introduction, the time is now right for going beyond sectarianism and ideology because there is less of a spirit of competition between different approaches, less of a spirit of "either your theory or mine" among those wanting to advance the science of psychotherapy. To go beyond sectarian-ism, however, may require us to accept that the different theoretical ap-proaches, like the different numerical systems, all refer to one reality. As the three examples in this chapter illustrate, focusing on what therapists *do* rather than on their brand of therapy may help to reveal that shared reality.

7

Concluding Remarks

I call it the problem of the "double-blind."
We cannot see that we don't see.
But if we see that we don't see,
Then we can see again.

Heinz von Foerster

When we mentioned to friends and acquaintances that we were writing a book on psychotherapy, we were often met with the question, "Do you believe psychotherapy works?" It was much the same tone of disbelief with which someone asks, "Do you believe therapy helps people?" if not quite "Do you believe people change?" But the critical question is not a matter of "believing in" therapy, it is a matter of accounting for what takes place when therapy works well.

Psychotherapy has often been viewed with more than a little skepticism and distrust. There are some who regard it as quackery rather than as a scientifically tested treatment form. Today, psychotherapy is coming under increasing scrutiny, facing tough questions about its effectiveness and practice. In an era of health care reform, employers and government planners are taking an even harder look at what therapy offers in exchange for limited dollars. Therapists are being required to justify every hour they spend in the consulting room.

In response to the growing demands for accountability, researchers have begun to amass a body of studies of therapy's effectiveness. The good news for professionals who practice or study psychotherapy is the studies show that most patients derive substantial benefits from psychotherapy. Studies show that therapy can make an important difference. Overall, most people who have been in therapy report some relief—improvements that made them less troubled and their lives more manageable.

Less successful, however, have been efforts to prove that some psychotherapies or techniques work better than others. Scientists have failed to prove the superiority of any major therapeutic school. Even in manualized studies, which are the most rigorous and best controlled, the results show no significant difference among different types of psychotherapy. These results come as a rude shock to efficacy researchers, since the main theme of efficacy studies has been the demonstration of the superiority of specific techniques for specific disorders.

What this means is that researchers and clinicians still do not understand what makes therapy effective. If no one technique can claim superiority, then by what process does improvement in psychotherapy operate? This has become the critical question. If we could understand the mechanisms by which psychotherapy works, we could undoubtedly know more about the process of human change and transformation. The great challenge has been to design methods that would explain these mechanisms.

There is no question that any therapy is a dyadic enterprise. In fact, researchers have shown that the strength of the therapeutic relationship is the most powerful predictor of psychotherapy outcome. Yet researchers have failed to provide precise descriptions of the inner workings of the therapeutic relationship. It is easy to suggest that a therapist should establish an "empathetic" or "warm" relationship with a patient, but it is much more difficult to define precisely which critical therapist behaviors will best achieve such a goal. A method that defines what patients and therapists do to establish a therapeutic relationship is still needed.

In chapter 5 we described what therapists actually do to establish a good therapeutic relationship. This means vaguer terms such as *empathy* or *warmth* can now be translated more meaningfully into specific therapists' behaviors. To state that a therapist matches a relation that a patient is assessing and induces the patient to assess it conditionally, after which the patient changes his or her assessment of that relation from reactive to selective—this is a more accurate description of a therapeutic interaction than a single dimensional description such as empathetic reflection. In the previous chapters we argued that this degree of descriptive specificity greatly enhances our ability to depict in-therapy performance. And it is these multi-dimensional descriptions of the process that will enable reliable description of phenomena at a level of clinical relevance.

We have tried to show that effective psychotherapy is not something mysterious, esoteric, or magical in which "anything goes." On the contrary, the process of successful psychotherapy follows a patterned set of behaviors. There is a direct relationship between what therapists do (or fail to do) during the process of therapy and outcome. The question of what takes place when psychotherapy works well may depend more on therapists than on therapies.

The practice of therapy rests on the assumption that looking inward has value, that the source of much "dysfunction" and unhappiness can be traced to the subjective world of emotions, thoughts, and perceptions.

Yet there are those such as Wendy Kaminer (1992), author of *I'm Dysfunctional, You're Dysfunctional,* who see therapy's emphasis on looking inward as encouraging a cult of victimhood. The flip side of self-reflection, she argues, is "selfhood" and "victimhood"—the tendency to interpret everything in individual, dysfunctional terms. The therapeutic culture encourages people to see themselves as victims rather than self-determining participants, Kaminer believes. One of the more reprehensible aspects of the therapeutic culture, in Kaminer's view, is that it offers absolution and no accountability. And instead of imposing the capacity to act, it confers entitlement to sympathy and support.

Similarly, Charles Sykes, author of *A Nation of Victims: The Decay of the American Character* (1992), sees therapy's emphasis on looking inward as the reason people are more concerned with justifying behavior than with finding solutions to the problems. Sykes argues that in place of evil, therapeutic society has substituted illness; in place of consequences, it urges understanding; in place of responsibility, it argues for a personality driven by impulses. Sykes believes that the illness excuse has become routine. Labeling all their problems symptoms of disease, people in therapy find external causes for what ails them, Sykes argues. In Sykes's view, dysfunction is a growth industry. The mantra of the victims is the same: "I am not responsible; it is not my fault."

Yet is it really *effective* psychotherapy that these writers bemoan? Or is it a distorted image of psychotherapy as reflected in pop culture—talk shows, weekend workshops, and fringe therapies? And do the criticisms collected here, egregious as they are, constitute evidence that all therapy encourages victimhood? Or is victimhood the result of an ineffective therapy?

Whereas contemporary culture reads into the message of psychotherapy the injunction to "feel good and embrace victimhood," effective therapy implores a radically different injunction. It is closer to George Kelly's (1955) injunction to "be ontologically responsible." When practiced well, Kelly says, therapy prods people to undertake increasing responsibility for their own actions, even those they may consider irrational or beyond their control.

Learning to assume such responsibility is a serious undertaking, Kelly argues, since it involves taking into one's own hands all the duties and problems of *making* one's own way in the world. Each person has to ask, Kelly says, "What ought he to be?"

The task of therapy, according to Kelly, is to provide means by which a person may attempt what previously would have seemed impossible. "What the therapist does is to invite the patient to envision new possibilities," Kelly says. This invitation is a difficult one, Kelly argues, because it invites the patient to see his or her situation in new and unfamiliar ways. Thus psychotherapy, according to Kelly, encourages people to feel anxiety as well as calmness, fear as well as security, pain as well as pleasure, and sadness as well as contentment.

In the previous chapters, we presented data that complement the theoretical work by Kelly, who has argued that effective therapy is related to the capacity of people to take responsibility for their behavior. Our findings showed that patients of a successful therapy accept their behavior as their own (internal) rather than seeing themselves as passive victims of their environment (reactive and external). They believe they have a choice in determining their behavior, can control their actions, and can exercise a certain amount of will (selective). By contrast, the findings showed that patients of an unsuccessful therapy are more likely to maintain external and reactive assessments.

When practiced well, we showed, therapy induces people to reassess their relationships and prods them to be more responsible for those assessments. The findings showed that therapists of a successful therapy were more likely to induce their patients to reassess their relationships (whereas therapists of an unsuccessful therapy tended toward information-seeking and instructive interactions). This higher level of induction in successful therapies and the data relating to the assessment of relations suggest that these two operations may be the way in which therapists of a successful therapy, as Kelly puts it, "create new possibilities for seeing things differently."

Heinz von Foerster (1985, p. 55) tells a story that metaphorically describes why learning to see things differently can be beneficial. The story is about a case brought to Dr. Victor Frankl, the neuropsychiatrist. In 1938, when the Nazis invaded Austria, Dr. Frankl and his family were arrested and sent to concentration camps. Frankl lost his entire family, but he survived and walked back to Vienna after the Allied troops had opened the gates of the camps.

Since he had suffered through the nadir of human experience, his presence in a city still occupied by foreign powers was very important. He helped many people who had suffered deeply from the experiences of the war.

In one case brought to Frankl, a husband and wife had, by miraculous circumstances, survived the Holocaust in two different concentration camps. They had met again in Vienna and couldn't believe they were both alive. However, the wife, after being reunited with her husband for a few months, died of a disease contracted in the camps. After that, the husband became completely despondent: he didn't want to eat any more, and he isolated himself and sat passively in a corner. Clearly, he had given up. Friends wanted to help him but he refused their assistance.

He was finally persuaded to see Frankl, and they talked to each other for an hour. At the end of their interaction Frankl made the following proposal to this man: "Assume that God would give me the power of producing a woman identical to your wife; she would remember all the details of your conversations, know the jokes and the experiences you had. You would not be able to see the difference, whatever test you gave her. You would see her like your wife. Would you like me to produce such a woman?" After a while, the man said, "No." Frankl said, "All right. Thank you." They separated. The man began to recover.

When von Foerster heard this story he asked Frankl, "What happened? What did you do?" Frankl replied, "It is quite clear. This man was seeing himself through the eyes of the other—through the eyes of his wife, but when she was dead, he was blind. When he could see that he was blind, he could see."

This idea that we are blind—that we see things not as they are, but as we are—has been discussed for a long time. Thousands of years ago, Epictetus said it is not the things themselves that trouble us, but the views that we have about these things. Generally we are unaware of our views, of the emotional values we give to our relations. As we mentioned in previous chapters, our relational assessments are implicit. Therapy, when practiced well, is a systematic way of inducing individuals to reassess the values they attribute to their relationships, thereby making their values explicit.

When effective therapists induce individuals to reassess their relations, they are, in essence, asking individuals to reassess the value they give to a relation. What turns out to be changed because of the reassessment is the meaning attributed to the relation, and therefore its consequences, but not its concrete facts—or, as Shakespeare expressed it, "There is nothing either good or bad, but thinking makes it so."

To reassess, then, means to change the emotional value (or conceptual value) in connection to which a relationship is experienced and to give it another value and thereby change its entire meaning. There is a reward to reassessment, and it travels a continuum—one that takes an individual through passive, blind assessments to awareness and active participation. A crucial difference between effective and ineffective therapy is the extent to which one's relational assessments are viewed in wider contexts. When practiced well, therapy means the whole development of an individual. It includes the reevaluation of his or her relational assessments and the refining of his or her emotional reactions.

In the case brought to Frankl, the husband assessed his attachment (closeness) to his wife positively. It was a miracle that both husband and wife survived the concentration camps. They lost everything during the war. They were probably the sole survivors of their extended families. It is reasonable to assume they had only each other. So this man, having lost everything, having suffered greatly, placed much value on his attachment to his wife. It was as if they were one person. It was a symbiotic devotion. When she died, however, he was forced to reassess his attachment. But he was unable to let go of his deep-felt attachment. He was unable to find new and transforming meaning in what remained of his life. Without his wife he felt his life had slipped away. When she died, he felt as if he lost himself, too.

Frankl prodded him to reassess the value he attributed to his attachment. Though the story fails to make obvious how Frankl did this, the outcome is made obvious. The man, we are told, saw that he was seeing the world through his wife's eyes. When he realized his devotion was causing him to see the world through her eyes, then he could reassess his attachment and change the meaning he attributed to his wife's death.

The death of a loved one is an event many of us have experienced. Some people when facing the death of a loved one can let go of their attachment.

Others may even face this event as an opportunity for major life changes. But for some people the loss is associated with debilitating mental and physical effects that may persist for years.

Since whatever value a person gives to a relational event is his or her responsibility, it contains the seed for an ethic. A seeming paradox of life is a person's power to create his or her own reality. As Kelly summed up the matter, the important question is not whether reality exists, it is what we make of it. What Kelly is suggesting is not naive optimism; rather, he suggests people may be limited primarily by the degree of their own ingenuity in exploring alternative possibilities of how they might understand things.

Psychotherapy, in this context, offers a chance to contribute to the improvement of human life. It seems to us, therefore, that to engage in such a human enterprise is a worthwhile venture. Although our attitude is positive, we know that the gap between ideal and reality in psychotherapy is large. Psychotherapy by itself cannot change society or lead it out of the wilderness. Our influence has to be circumscribed. We can help people change their assessments, but we cannot change their character. We cannot eradicate racism, or poverty, or war. Psychotherapy cannot be a miracle transformation or a paradise cure in a sea of discontent.

But modesty and realism concerning the capacities of psychotherapy do not in any sense imply that a therapist's role in determining the quality of a person's life is small. Therapy eases the problems that people bring to treatment. It helps them function better, improving their ability to relate well to others, to be productive at work, and to cope with everyday stress. And it enhances what can be called "personal growth." People in therapy have more confidence and self-esteem, understand themselves better, and enjoy life more.

To our many critics we say: your warnings of the hazards of gazing within have not altered the fact there are many people with serious psychological problems whose effective treatment still awaits the accumulation of greater knowledge. To ourselves we say: to gain that knowledge requires a continued and difficult effort, and the task remains as one of the most important to face the researcher and the clinician.

We trust that our effort in this book toward defining effective treatment in empirical terms is a step toward improving our ability to specify what is expected of competent therapists and methods for evaluating a particular therapist's competence. We are confident that it is now possible to define effective performance in terms of how the therapeutic process is managed. In contrast to the traditional model of focusing on theories or techniques, we have tried to show that attention must also be given to what therapists actually do.

We hope readers enjoy the glimpses into our research, question its conclusions thoughtfully, and test the implications in their own lives. "Good" conclusions are good only as far as they inspire questions for new beginnings. So we hope the work reported here will serve as a useful point of departure for future work, both empirical and theoretical.

Appendix: List of Relationships

People assess relationships along contrasting poles—for example, closeness or distance, autonomy or complementarity, spontaneity or deliberateness, stability or instability. People also assess the value of each pole as either negative or positive. For example, a close relationship can be assessed as intrusive versus intimate; a distant relationship as uninvolved versus private; a spontaneous relationship as impulsive versus carefree; a deliberate relationship as rigid versus planned; and so on. The following is a list (adapted from the work of Katsenelinboigen and Schultz) of the bipolar relational categories with examples of positive and negative assessments.

Pole A	Pole B
Compatibility: Ability to get along	**Incompatibility:** Inability to get along
[+] "He is very sociable."	[+] "She is a nonconformist."
[−] "He is a pliant person."	[−] "He is argumentative."
Equality: Equivalency of positions	**Dominance:** Superiority of position
[+] "We share all the household tasks."	[+] "He is a good leader."
[−] "Everything I do he wants to do."	[−] "She bosses me around."
Monopolization: Possession or control	**Influencelessness:** Inability to have possession or control
[+] "He is the decision maker."	[+] "He is an objective observer."
[−] "She runs my life."	[−] "Nothing I do turns out the way I want it to."
Divergence: Motion away from a common point	**Convergence:** Motion toward a common point
[+] "He likes debating."	[+] "He is a peacemaker."
[−] "He is oppositional."	[−] "She is a nepotist."
Excreticity: Openness to outputs	**Retentionness:** Lack of openness to outputs
[+] "She is very expressive about her feelings."	[+] "He is a man who measures his words."
[−] "He is a chatterbox."	[−] "She is very withdrawn."

Unilaterality: Exchange in one direction
[+] "He is charitable and altruistic."
[−] "She is an exploiter."

Permeability: Open boundaries
[+] "She is very concerned."
[−] "He is very intrusive."

Complementarity: Ability to work together as a unit
[+] "They work as a team."
[−] "They are co-dependent."

Proximity: Nearness
[+] "She is a loving person."
[−] "She is a clingy person."

Reflecticity: Tendency to examine oneself
[+] "She is introspective."
[−] "He is self-absorbed."

Sensitiveness: Tendency to react to an external force
[+] "He is very sympathetic."
[−] "She is so touchy."

Consistency: Lack of contradictions or opposing qualities
[+] "He is loyal."
[−] "She is so blunt."

Stationarity: Tendency toward a stable course
[+] "He is very steady."
[−] "He is stubborn."

Maturity: Showing differentiation or development
[+] "He is seasoned."
[−] "She is overly responsible."

Explorability: Tendency to search for new ways
[+] "He is innovative."
[−] "She is self-indulgent."

Reciprocity: Exchange in both directions
[+] "She always returns the favor."
[−] "One hand washes the other."

Closedness: Closed boundaries
[+] "She is a very private person."
[−] "She is like a watchdog."

Autonomy: Ability to work independently
[+] "He is self-reliant."
[−] "She is uncommitted."

Distance: Remoteness or separation
[+] "He is reserved."
[−] "He is cold and indifferent."

Irreflecticity: Disinclination to examine oneself
[+] "She is spontaneous."
[−] "He is impulsive."

Irresponsiveness: Lack of reaction to external force
[+] "She is a composed person."
[−] "He is unappreciative."

Inconsistency: Tendency toward contradictions or opposing qualities
[+] "She is a complex person."
[−] "She is a deceitful person."

Mobility: Tendency to change course

[+] "He is very original."
[−] "He is erratic."

Immaturity: Lack of differentiation or development
[+] "He is very innocent."
[−] "She is inexperienced and naive."

Conservativeness: Tendency to maintain customary ways
[+] "He is cautious."
[−] "He is old-fashioned."

Reversibility: Ability to return to a previous state
[+] "He does not bear a grudge."
[−] "She is fickle."

Irreversibility: Inability to return to a previous state
[+] "He is persevering."
[−] "He is unforgiving."

References

Abramson, L., Seligman, M., & Teasdale, J. (1978). Learned helplessness in humans: Critique and reformulation. *Journal of Abnormal Psychology, 87,* 49–74.

Arkowitz, H. (1992). Integrative theories of therapy. In D. Freedheim (Ed.), *History of psychotherapy: A century of change* (pp. 261–303). Washington, DC: American Psychological Association.

Austin, J. L. (1962). *How to do things with words.* Cambridge: Harvard University Press.

Bachelor, A. (1990, June). *Comparison and relationship to outcome of diverse dimensions of the helping alliance as seen by client and therapist.* Paper presented at the meeting of the Society for Psychotherapy Research, Wintergreen, Va.

Bakeman, R., & Gottman, J. (1986). *Observing interactions: An introduction to sequential analysis.* Cambridge: Cambridge University Press.

Bandura, A. (1969). *Principles of behavior modification.* New York: Holt, Rinehart & Winston.

———. (1977). Self-efficacy: Toward a unifying theory of behavioral change. *Psychological Review, 84,* 191–215.

———. (1989). Human agency in social cognitive theory. *American Psychologist, 44,* 1175–84.

Barnard, C. (1968). *The functions of the executive.* Cambridge: Harvard University Press (first published 1936).

Baron, R. M., & Boudreau, L. A. (1987). An ecological perspective on integrating personality and social psychology. *Journal of Personality and Social Psychology, 53,* 1222–28.

Bassili, J. (1976). Temporal and spatial contingencies in the perception of social events. *Journal of Personality and Social Psychology, 33,* 680–85.

Beck, A. (1967). *Depression: Causes and Treatment.* Philadelphia: University of Pennsylvania.

———. (1978). Demonstration of the cognitive therapy of depression: The first interview. Unpublished manuscript, University of Pennsylvania.

———. (1985). Cognitive therapy. In J. Zeig (Ed.), *The evolution of psychotherapy* (pp. 143–56). New York: Brunner Mazel.

Beck, A., Rush, A., Shaw, B., & Emery, G. (1979). *Cognitive therapy of depression: A treatment manual.* New York: Guilford.

Bergin, A. E. (1982). *Comment on converging themes in psychotherapy.* New York: Springer.

Bergin, A. E., & Strupp, H. (1970). New directions in psychotherapy research. *Journal of Abnormal Psychology, 76,* 13–26.

———. (1972). *Changing frontiers in the science of psychotherapy.* New York: Aldine-Atherton.

Beutler, L. E. (1983). *Eclectic psychotherapy: A systematic approach.* New York: Pergamon.

Bordin, E. (1975, June). *The generalizability of the psychoanalytic concept of working alliance.* Paper presented at the annual meeting of the Society for Psychotherapy Research, Boston.

———. (1976, September). *The working alliance: Basis for a general theory of psychotherapy.* Paper presented at the annual meeting for the American Psychological Association, Washington, DC.

———. (1980, June). *Of human bonds that bind or free.* Paper presented at the annual meeting of the Society for Psychotherapy Research, Pacific Grove, CA.

Brady, J. P., Davison, G. C., DeWald, P. A., Egan, G., Fadiman, J., Frank, J. D., Gill, M. M., Hoffman, I., Kempler, W., Lazarus, A. A., Raimy, V., Rotter, J. B., & Strupp, H. H. (1980). Some views on effective principles of psychotherapy. *Cognitive Therapy and Research, 4,* 269–306.

Breuer, J., & Freud, S. (1957). *Studies on hysteria.* New York: Basic (original work published in 1895).

Bruner, J. (1986). *Actual minds, possible worlds.* Cambridge: Harvard University Press.

———. (1990). *Acts of meaning.* Cambridge: Harvard University Press.

Brunink, S., & Schroeder, H. (1979). Verbal therapeutic behavior of expert psychoanalytically oriented, Gestalt, and behavior therapists. *Journal of Consulting and Clinical Psychology, 47,* 567–74.

Chase, W., & Simon, H. (1973). Perception in chess. *Cognitive Psychology, 4,* 55–81.

Chi, M. T. H., Feltovich, P. J., & Glaser, R. (1981). Categorization and representation of physics problems by experts and novices. *Cognitive Science, 5,* 121–52.

Chinsky, J. M., & Rappaport, J. (1970). Brief-critique of meaning and reliability of "accurateempathy" ratings. *Psychological Bulletin, 73,* 379–82.

Cornsweet, C. (1983). Nonspecific factors and theoretical choice. *Psychotherapy: Theory, Research, and Practice, 20,* 307–13.

Cross, D. G., Sheehan, P. W., & Kahan, J. A. (1982). Short- and long-term follow-up of clients receiving insight-oriented and clinical psychology. *Journal of Consulting and Clinical Psychology, 50,* 103–12.

Dantzig, T. (1954). *Number: The language of science.* New York: Free Press.

Denker, R. (1946). Results of treatment of psychoneuroses by the general practitioner. A follow-up study of 500 cases. *New York State Journal of Medicine, 46,* 2164–66.

Docherty, J. (1985). Introduction to section V (The therapeutic alliance and treatment outcome). In R. Hales & A. Frances (Eds.), *APA Annual Review* (vol. 4, pp. 527–31). Washington, DC: American Psychiatric Press.

Duncan, B. L. (1992). Strategic therapy, eclecticism, and the therapeutic relationship. *Journal of Marital and Family Therapy, 18,* 17–23.

Edelson, M. (1994). Can psychotherapy research answer this psychotherapist's questions? In F. Talley, H. Strupp, & S. Butler (Eds.), *Psychotherapy Research and Practice* (pp. 60–88). New York: Basic.

Elkin, I. (1994). The NIMH Treatment of Depression Collaborative Research Program: Where we began and where we are. In A. Bergin & S. Garfield (Eds.), *Handbook of psychotherapy and behavior change* (4th ed.) (pp. 114–39). New York: Wiley.

Elkin, I., Parloff, M., Hadley, S., & Autry, J. (1985). NIMH treatment of depression collaborative research program. *Archives of General Psychiatry, 42,* 305–16.

Elkin, I., Pilkonis, P., Docherty, J., & Sotsky, S. (1988). Conceptual and methodological issues in comparative studies of psychotherapy and pharmacotherapy, I: Active ingredients and mechanisms of change. *The American Journal of Psychiatry, 145,* 909–17.

Elkin, I., Shea, T., Watkins, J., Imber, S., Sotsky, S., Collins, J., Glass, D., Pilkonis, P., Leber, W., Docherty, J., Fiester, S., & Parloff, M. (1989). National Institute of Mental Health Treatment of depression collaborative research program. *Archives of General Psychiatry, 46,* 971–82.

Elliott, R., & Anderson, C. (1994). Simplicity and complexity in psychotherapy research. In R. Russell (Ed.), *Reassessing psychotherapy research* (pp. 65–113). New York: Guilford.

Ellis, A. (1984). Is the unified-interaction approach to cognitive-behavior modification a reinvention of the wheel? *Clinical Psychological Review, 4,* 215–18.

Erikson, E. (1964). *Insight and responsibility.* New York: Norton.

Eysenck, H. J. (1952). The effects of psychotherapy: An evaluation. *Journal of Consulting Psychology, 16,* 319–24.

Feifel, H., & Eells, J. (1963). Patients and therapists assess the same psychotherapy. *Journal of Consulting Psychology, 27,* 310–17.

Foerster, H. von. (1985). To know and to let know: An applied theory of knowledge. *Cybernetics, 1,* 47–55.

Forsterling, F. (1985). Attributional training: A review. *Psychological Bulletin, 98,* 495–512.

———. (1986). Attributional conceptions in clinical psychology. *American Psychologist, 41,* 275–85.

Frank, A. F., & Gunderson, J. G. (1990). The role of the therapeutic alliance in the treatment of schizophrenia. *Archives of General Psychiatry, 47,* 228–36.

Frank, J. D. (1961). *Persuasion and healing.* Baltimore: Johns Hopkins University Press.

———. (1978). Expectations and therapeutic outcome: The placebo effect and the role induction interview. In J. D. Frank, R. Hoehn-Saric, S. D. Imber, B. L. Liberman, & A. R. Stone (Eds.), *Effective ingredients of successful psychotherapy* (2d ed.) (pp. 1–34). New York: Brunner Mazel.

———. (1982). Therapeutic components shared by all psychotherapies. In J. H.

Harvey and M. M. Parks (Eds.), *The Master Lecture Series*. Vol. 1, *Psychotherapy research and behavior change* (pp. 73–122). Washington, DC: American Psychological Association.

Freud, S. (1959). On psychotherapy. In E. Jones (Ed.), *Collected Papers* (vol. 1, pp. 249–64). New York: Basic (original published in 1904).

———. (1963). Introductory lectures in psychoanalysis. In J. Strachey (Ed. and Trans.), *The standard edition of the complete psychological works of Sigmund Freud* (vol. 16, pp. 241–489). London: Hogarth (original published in 1917).

———. (1964). New introductory lectures on psychoanalysis. In J. Strachey (Ed. and Trans.), *The standard edition of the complete psychological works of Sigmund Freud* (vol. 22, pp. 1–182). London: Hogarth (original published in 1933).

———. (1966a). The dynamics of the transference. In J. Strachey (Ed. and Trans.), *The standard edition of the complete psychological works of Sigmund Freud* (vol. 12, pp. 99–108). London: Hogarth (originally published in 1912).

———. (1966b). On beginning the treatment. In J. Strachey (Ed. and Trans.), *The standard edition of the complete psychological works of Sigmund Freud* (vol. 12, pp. 112–44). London: Hogarth (original published in 1913).

Frieswyk, S., Allen, J., Colson, D., Coyne, L., Gabbard, G., Horwitz, L., & Newsom, G. (1986). Therapeutic alliance: Its place as a process and outcome variable in dynamic psychotherapy research. *Journal of Consulting and Clinical Psychology, 54*, 32–38.

Garfield, S. L. (1980). *Psychotherapy: An eclectic approach.* New York: Wiley.

Garfield, S. L., & Bergin, A. (1986). Introduction and historical overview. In S. L. Garfield & A. E. Bergin (Eds.), *Handbook of psychotherapy and behavior change* (3d ed., pp. 3–23). New York: Wiley.

Giacomo, D., & Weissmark, M. (1986). Systemic practice. *Family Process, 25*, 483–512.

———. (1987). A generative theory of the therapeutic field. *Family Process, 26*, 437–59.

———. (1992a). How psychotherapy works. *The Psychiatric Times, 10*, 27–28.

———. (1992b). Mechanisms of action in psychotherapy. *Journal of Psychotherapy Practice and Research. 1*, 37–48.

Goldfried, M. R. (1980). Toward the delineation of therapeutic change principles. *American Psychologist, 35*, 991–99.

——— (Ed.). (1982). *Converging themes in psychotherapy.* New York: Springer.

Goldstein, A., Heller, K., & Sechrest, L. (1966). *Psychotherapy and the psychology of behavior change.* New York: Wiley.

Gomes-Schwartz, B. (1978). Effective ingredients in psychotherapy: Prediction of outcome from process variables. *Journal of Consulting and Clinical Psychology, 46*, 1023–35.

Gormally, J., & Hill, C. E. (1974). Guidelines for research on Carkuff's model. *Journal of Counseling Psychology, 21*, 539–47.

Gottman, J., Markman, H., & Notarius, C. (1977). The topography of marital conflict: A sequential analysis of verbal and nonverbal behavior. *Journal of Marriage and the Family, 39,* 461–77.

Greenberg, J. (1994). Psychotherapy research: A clinician's view. In F. Talley, H. Strupp, & S. Butler (Eds.), *Psychotherapy research and practice* (pp. 1–18). New York: Basic.

Greenberg, L. S. (1986). Research strategies. In L. S. Greenberg & W. M. Pinsof (Eds.), *The psychotherapeutic process: A research handbook* (pp. 707–31). New York: Guilford.

Greenberg, L. S., & Pinsof, W. M. (Eds.). (1986). *The psychotherapeutic process: A research handbook.* New York: Guilford.

Greenberg, L. S., & Webster, M. C. (1982). Resolving decisional conflict by Gestalt two-chair dialogue: Relating process to outcome. *Journal of Counseling Psychology, 29,* 468–77.

Grencavage, L., & Norcross, J. (1990). Where are the commonalities among the therapeutic common factors? *Professional Psychology: Research & Practice, 21,* 372–78.

Gurman, A. S. (1980). Behavioral marital therapy in the 1980's: The challenge of integration. *American Journal of Family Therapy, 8,* 86–96.

Haaga, D. A. (1986). A review of the common principles approach to the integration of psychotherapies. *Cognitive Therapy and Research, 10,* 527–38.

Hammond, K. R. (1955). Probabilistic functioning and the clinical method. *Psychological Review, 67,* 411–526.

Hansell, J. (1990, June). *The relationship of the California Psychotherapy alliance scales to other measures of the alliance.* Paper presented at the meeting of the Society for Psychotherapy Research, Wintergreen, VA.

Hartley, D. (1985). Research on the therapeutic alliance in psychotherapy. In *APA Annual Review,* vol 4. Washington, DC: American Psychiatric Press.

Hartley, D., & Strupp, H. (1983). The therapeutic alliance: Its relationship to outcome in brief psychotherapy. In J. Maslinh (Ed.), *Empirical studies of psychoanalytic theories* (pp. 1–37). Hillsdale, NJ: Erlbaum.

Havens, L. (1986). *Making contact: Uses of language in psychotherapy.* Cambridge: Harvard University Press.

———. (1994). Some suggestions for making research more applicable to clinical practice. In F. Talley, H. Strupp, & S. Butler (Eds.), *Psychotherapy research and practice* (pp. 60–88). New York: Basic.

Heatherington, L. (1990). Family therapy, control, and controllingness. *Journal of Family Psychology, 4,* 132–50.

Hebb, D. O. (1946). Emotion in man and animal: An analysis of the intuitive processes of recognition. *Psychological Review, 53,* 88–106.

Heider, F. (1958). *The psychology of interpersonal relations.* New York: Wiley.

Heider, F., & Simmel, M. (1944). Social perception and phenomenal causality. *Psychological Review, 51,* 358–74.

Henry, W., Strupp, H., Butler, S., Schacht, T., & Binder, J. (1993). Effects of training in time-limited dynamic psychotherapy: Changes in therapist behavior. *Journal of Consulting and Clinical Psychology, 61,* 434–40.

Hersen, M., & Barlow, D. (1976). *Single-case experimental designs: Strategies for studying behavior change*. New York: Pergamon.

Hill, C., O'Grady, K., & Elkin, R. (1992). Applying the collaborative study psychotherapy rating scale to rate therapist adherence in cognitive-behavior therapy, interpersonal therapy, and clinical management. *Journal of Consulting & Clinical Psychology, 60,* 73–79.

Hoffman, L. (1985). Beyond power and control: Toward a second-order family systems therapy. *Family Systems Medicine, 3,* 381–96.

Horowitz, M., & Marmar, C. (1985). The therapeutic alliance with difficult patients. *Psychiatry Update Annual Review, 4,* 573–84.

Horvath, A., Greenberg, L. (1986). The development of the working alliance inventory. In L. S. Greenberg & W. M. Pinsof (Eds.), *The psychotherapeutic process: A research handbook* (pp. 529–57). New York: Guilford.

Horvath, A., & Greenberg, L. S. (1989). The development and validation of the Working Alliance Inventory. *Journal of Counseling Psychology, 36,* 223–33.

Horvath, A., & Luborsky, L. (1993). The role of the therapeutic alliance in psychotherapy. *Journal of Consulting and Clinical Psychology, 61,* 561–73.

Horvath, A., & Marx, R. (1991). The development and decay of the working alliance during time-limited counseling. *Canadian Journal of Counseling, 24,* 240–59.

Horvath, A., & Symonds, D. (1991). Relation between working alliance and outcome in psychotherapy: A met-analysis. *Journal of Counseling Psychology, 38,* 139–49.

Howard, K., Lueger, R., Mailing, M., & Martinovich, Z. (1993). A phase model of psychotherapy outcome: Causal mediation of change. *Journal of Consulting and Clinical Psychology, 61,* 678–85.

Hyman, R., & Breger, L. (1965). Discussion in H. J. Eysenck, The effects of psychotherapy.

International Journal of Psychiatry, 1, 317–322.

Izard, C., Kagan, J., & Zajonc, R. (1984). Introduction. In C. Izard, J. Kagan, & R. Zajonc, (Eds.), *Emotions, cognition, and behavior* (pp. 1–17). Cambridge: Cambridge University Press.

Jones, E., Cumming, J. D., & Horowitz, M. J. (1988). Another look at the nonspecific hypothesis of therapeutic effectiveness. *Journal of Clinical and Consulting Psychology, 56,* 48–55.

Jones, E., & Pulos, S. (1993). Comparing the process in psychodynamic and cognitive-behavioral therapies. *Journal of Consulting and Clinical Psychology, 61,* 306–16.

Kagan, J. (1989). *Unstable ideas: Temperament, cognition, and self*. Cambridge: Harvard University Press.

Kagan, J., & Segal, J. (1968). *Psychology : An introduction* (6th ed.). Orlando, FL: Harcourt Brace Jovanovich.

Kaminer, W. (1992). *I'm dysfunctional, you're dysfunctional*. New York: Vintage.

Karasu, T. (1986). The specificity versus nonspecificity dilemma: Toward identifying therapeutic change agents. *The American Journal of Psychiatry, 143:6,* 687–95.

Katsenelinboigen, A. (1984). *Some new trends in systems theory.* Seaside, CA: Intersystems Publications.

Kazdin, A. (1986). The evaluation of psychotherapy: Research design and methodology. In S. L. Garfield & A. E. Bergin (Eds.), *Handbook of psychotherapy and behavior change* (3d ed., pp. 23–68). New York: Wiley.

———. (1994). Methodology, design, and evaluation in psychotherapy research. In A. E. Bergin & S. L. Garfield (Eds.), *Handbook of psychotherapy and behavior change* (4th ed., pp. 19–71). New York: Wiley.

Kazdin, A., & Wilson, G. (1978). *Evaluation of behavior therapy: Issues, evidence, and research strategies.* Cambridge, MA: Ballinger.

Kelly, G. (1955). *The psychology of personal constructs.* New York: Norton.

Klerman, G., Rounsaville, B., Chevron, E., Neu, C., & Weissman, M. (1984). *Manual for short-term interpersonal therapy for depression.* New York: Basic.

Kokotovic, A. M., & Tracey, T. J. (1990). Working alliance in the early phase of counseling. *Journal of Counseling Psychology, 37,* 16–21.

Kraepelin, E. (1883). *Compedium der psychiatrie.* Leipzig: Abel.

Krupnick, J. (1988). *A comparative analysis of the therapeutic alliance in four brief treatments for depression.* Unpublished doctoral dissertation, University of Maryland.

Kuhn, T. (1977). Second thoughts on paradigms. In *The essential tension* (p. 305). Chicago: University of Chicago Press.

Lambert, M. (1986). Implications of psychotherapy outcome research for eclectic psychotherapy. In J. C. Norcross (Ed.), *Handbook of eclectic psychotherapy* (pp. 436–62). New York: Brunner Mazel.

Lambert, M., DeJulio, S., & Stein, D. (1978). Therapist interpersonal skills: Process, outcome, methodological considerations, and recommendations for future research. *Psychological Bulletin, 85,* 467–89.

Lambert, M., Shapiro, D., & Bergin, A. (1986). The effectiveness of psychotherapy. In S. L. Garfield & A. E. Bergin (Eds.), *Handbook of psychotherapy and behavior change* (3d ed., pp. 157–213). New York: Wiley.

Landis, C. (1938). A statistical evaluation of psychotherapeutic methods. In S. E. Hinsie (Ed.), *Concepts and problems of psychotherapy* (pp. 155–69). London: Heinemann.

Langer, E. (1983). *The psychology of control.* Beverly Hills, CA: Sage.

———. (1989). *Mindfulness.* New York: Addison Wesley.

Langer, E., & Rodin, J. (1977). Long-term effects of a control relevant intervention among the institutionalized aged. *Journal of Personality and Social Psychology, 35,* 897–902.

Lazarus, A. A. (1971). *Behavior therapy and beyond.* New York: McGraw-Hill.

Lazarus, R. (1991). *Emotion and adaptation.* Oxford: Oxford University Press.

Lazarus, R., & Smith, C. (1988). Knowledge and appraisal in the cognition-emotion relationship. *Cognition and Emotion, 2,* 281–300.

LeDoux, J. E. (1989). Cognitive-emotional interactions in the brain. *Cognition and Emotion, 3,* 267–89.

Leitner, L. M. (1982). Literalism, perspectivisim, chaotic fragmentalism and psychotherapy techniques. *British Journal of Medical Psychology, 55,* 307–17.

Light, R. (1990). *The Harvard assessment seminars: First report.* Cambridge: Harvard University.

Llewelyn, S. P., & Hume, W. J. (1979). The patient's view of therapy. *British Journal of Medical Psychology, 52,* 29–36.

Luborsky, L. (1976). Helping alliance in psychotherapy. In J. L. Cleghorn (Ed.), *Successful Psychotherapy* (pp. 92–116). New York: Brunner Mazel.

———. (1984). *Principles of psychodynamic psychotherapy.* New York: Basic.

Luborsky, L., & Crits-Christoph, P. (1990). *Understanding transference: The core conflictual relationship theme method.* New York: Basic.

Luborsky, L., Singer, B., & Luborsky, Lise. (1975). Comparative studies of psychotherapies: Is it true that "everyone has won and all must have prizes"? *Archives of General Psychiatry, 32,* 995–1008.

Luborsky, L., Woody, G. E., McLellan, A. T., O'Brien, C. P., & Rosenzweig, J. (1982). Can independent judges recognize different psychotherapies? An experience with manual guided therapies. *Journal of Consulting and Clinical Psychology, 50,* 49–62.

Luchins, A. (1942). Mechanization in problem solving. The effect of Einstellung. *Psychological Monographs, 54* (6, whole no. 248).

Maher, B. (1991). A personal history of clinical psychology. In M. Hersen, A. Kazdin, & A. Bellack (Eds.), *The clinical psychology handbook* (2d ed., pp. 3–25). New York: Pergamon.

Marmar, C., Weiss, D. S., & Gaston, L. (1989). Toward the validation of the California Therapeutic Alliance Rating System. *Psychological Assessment: A Journal of Consulting and Clinical Psychology, 1,* 46–52.

Marziali, E. (1984). Three viewpoints on the therapeutic alliance scales similarities, differences and associations with psychotherapy outcome. *Journal of Nervous and Mental Disease, 172,* 417–23.

Merleau-Ponty, M. (1962). *Phenomenology of perception* (C. Smith, Trans.). London: Routledge & Kegan Paul.

Michotte, A. E. (1950). The emotions regarded as functional connections. In M. Reymert (Ed.), *Feelings and emotions* (pp. 114–26). New York: McGraw-Hill.

Minuchin, S., & Fishman, C. (1981). *Family Therapy Thechniques.* Cambridge: Harvard University Press.

Mischel, W. (1990). Personality dispositions revisited and revised: A view after three decades. In L. A. Pervin (Ed.), *Handbook of Personality* (pp. 111–32). New York: Guilford.

Mitchell, K., Bozarth, J., & Krauft, C. (1977). A reappraisal of the therapeutic effectiveness of accurate empathy, nonpossessive warmth, and genuineness. In A. S. Gurman & A. M. Razin (Eds.), *Effective psychotherapy: A handbook of research.* New York: Pergamon.

Murray, H. (1938). *Explorations in Personality.* New York: Oxford University Press.

Orlinsky, D., & Howard, K. (1986). Process and outcome in psychotherapy. In S. L. Garfield & A. E. Bergin (Eds.), *Handbook of psychotherapy and behavior change* (3d ed., pp. 311–81). New York: Wiley.

————. (1987). A generic model of psychotherapy. *Journal of Integrative and Eclectic Psychotherapy, 6,* 6–27.

Ortony, A. (1979). Metaphor: A multidimensional problem. In A. Ortony (Ed.), *Metaphor and Thought* (pp. 1–18). Cambridge: Cambridge University Press.

Ortony, A., Clore, G., & Collins, A. (1988). *The cognitive structure of emotions.* Cambridge: Cambridge University Press.

Parloff, M. B., & Dies, R. R. (1977). Group psychotherapy outcome research 1966–1975. *International Journal of Group Psychotherapy, 27,* 281–319.

Parloff, M. B., Waskow, I. E., Wolfe, B. E. (1978). Research of therapist variables in relation to process and outcome. In S. L. Garfield & A. E. Bergin (Eds.), *Handbook of psychotherapy and behavior change: An empirical analysis* (2d ed., pp. 233–82). New York: Wiley.

Piaget, J. (1972). *Psychology of intelligence.* Totowa, NJ: Adams.

Polanyi, M. (1958). *Personal knowledge: Towards a post-critical philosophy.* Chicago: The University of Chicago Press.

Prochaska, J. O. (1984). *Systems of psychotherapy: A transtheoretical analysis* (2d ed.). Homewood, IL: Dorsey.

Prochaska, J. O., & DiClemente, C. C. (1986). The transtheoretical approach. In J. C. Norcross (Ed.), *Handbook of eclectic psychotherapy* (pp. 163–200). New York: Brunner Mazel.

Rachman, S. J., & Wilson, G. T. (1980). *The effects of psychological therapy* (2d ed). New York: Pergamon.

Rosenblatt, A., & Thikstun, J. (1977). Modern psychoanalytic concepts in a general psychology. *Psychological Issues, XI,* Monograph 42/43.

Rosenthal, R. (1983). Assessing the statistical and social importance of the effects of psychotherapy. *Journal of Consulting and Clinical Psychology, 51,* 4–13.

Rosenthal, R., & Rubin, D. B. (1982). A simple general purpose display of magnitude of experimental effect. *Journal of Educational Psychology, 74,* 166–69.

Rosenzweig, S. (1936). Some implicit common factors in diverse methods of psychotherapy. *American Journal of Orthopsychiatry, 6,* 422–25.

Rosnow, R., & Rosenthal, R. (1989). Statistical procedures and the justification of knowledge in Psychological Science. *American Psychologist, 44,* 1276–84.

Rounsaville, B., Chevron, E., Prusof, B., Elkin, I., Imber, S., Sotsky, S., & Watkins, J. (1987). The relation between specific and general dimensions of the psychotherapy process in interpersonal psychotherapy of depression. *Journal of Consulting and Clinical Psychology, 55,* 379–84.

Rounsaville, B., Chevron, E., Weissman, M., Prusoff, B., & Frank, E. (1986). Training therapists to perform interpersonal psychotherapy in clinical trials. *Comprehensive Psychiatry, 27,* 364–71.

Ryle, A. (1978). A common language for psychotherapies? *British Journal of Psychiatry, 132,* 585–94.

———. (1982). *Psychotherapy: A cognitive integration of therapy and practice.* London: Academic.

———. (1984). How can we compare different psychotherapies? Why are they all effective? *British Journal of Medical Psychology, 57,* 261–64.

Saburin, S., Hansell, J., Gutfreund, J., Gaston, L., & Marmar, C. R. (1990, June). *Reliability and validity of the three versions of the California Psychotherapy Alliances Scales (CALPAS).* Paper presented at the meeting of the Society for Psychotherapy Research, Wintergreen, VA.

Safran, J., Crocker, P., McMain, S., & Murray, P. (1990). The therapeutic alliance rupture as a therapy event for empirical investigation. *Psychotherapy, 27:* 154–65.

Schaffer, N. D. (1982). Multidimensional measures of therapist behavior as predictors of outcome. *Psychological Bulletin, 92,* 670–81.

Schön, D. (1983). *The reflective practitioner: How professionals think in action.* New York: Basic.

Seligman, M. (1975). *Helplessness: On depression, development and death.* San Francisco: Freeman.

Senger, H. (1994). Personal communication.

Shapiro, A. K. (1971). Placebo effects in medicine, psychotherapy, and psychoanalysis. In A. E. Bergin & S. L. Garfield (Eds.), *Handbook of psychotherapy and behavior change* (3d ed., pp. 439–73).

Shapiro, D. A. (1976). The effects of therapeutic conditions: Positive results revisited. *British Journal of Medical Psychology, 49,* 213–323.

Shapiro, D. A., Startup, M., Bird, D., Harper, H., Reynolds, S., & Suokas, A. (1994). The high-water mark of the drug metaphor: A meta-analytic critique of process-outcome research. In R. L. Russell (Ed.), *Reassessing Psychotherapy Research* (pp. 1–35). New York: Guilford.

Shepard, R. (1984). Ecological constraints on internal representations: Resonant kinematics of perceiving, imagining, thinking, and dreaming. *Psychological Review, 91,* 417–47.

Silberschatz, G., & Curtis, J. (1993). Measuring the therapist's impact on the patient's therapeutic progress. *Journal of Consulting and Clinical Psychology, 61,* 403–11.

Simon, H. (1983). *Reason in human affairs.* Stanford, CA: Stanford University Press.

Sloane, R. B., Staples, F. R., Cristol, A. H., Yorkson, N.J., & Whipple, K. (1975). *Psychotherapy versus behavior therapy.* Cambridge: Harvard University Press.

Smith, M. L., & Glass, G. V. (1977). Meta-analysis of psychotherapy outcome studies. *American Psychologist, 32,* 752–60.

Smith, M. L., Glass, G. V., & Miller, T. I. (1980). *The benefits of psychotherapy.* Baltimore: Johns Hopkins University Press.

Sticht, T. (1979). Educational uses of metaphor. In A. Ortony (Ed.), *Metaphor and thought* (pp. 474–85). Cambridge: Cambridge University Press.

Stiles, W., Shapiro, D., & Elliott, R. (1986). Are all psychotherapies equivalent? *American Psychologist, 41,* 165–80.

Stotland, E., & Blumenthal, A. L. (1964). The reduction of anxiety as a result of the expectation of making a choice. *Canadian Review of Psychology, 18,* 139–45.

Strupp, H., Fox, R. E., & Lessler, K. J. (1969). *Patients view their psychotherapy.* Baltimore: Johns Hopkins University Press.

Strupp, H., & Hadley, S. (1979). Specific versus nonspecific factors in psychotherapy: A controlled study of outcome. *Archives of General Psychiatry, 36,* 1125–36.

Strupp, H., & Luborsky, L. (Eds.). (1962). *Research in psychotherapy,* vol. 2. Washington, DC: American Psychological Association.

Sullivan, H. (1940). *Conceptions of modern psychiatry.* New York: Norton.

Sykes, C. (1992). *A nation of victims.* New York: St. Martin's.

Tichenor, V., & Hill, C. E. (1989). A comparison of six measures of working alliance. *Psychotherapy: Research and Practice, 26,* 195–99.

Toates, F. (1986). *Motivational systems.* Cambridge: Cambridge University Press.

Trevarthen, C. (1979). Communication and cooperation in early infancy: A description of primary intersubjectivity. In M. Bullowa (Ed.), *Before speech: The beginnings of primary communication.* Cambridge: Cambridge University Press.

Truax, C. B., & Carkhuff, R. R. (1967). *Toward effective counseling and psychotherapy.* Chicago: Aldine.

Tukey, J. (1977). *Exploratory data analysis.* Reading, MA: Addison-Wesley.

Urban, H., & Ford, D. (1971). Some historical and conceptual perspectives on psychotherapy and behavior change. In S. L. Garfield & A. E. Bergin (Eds.), *Handbook of psychotherapy and behavior change* (pp. 3–35). New York: Wiley.

Watzlawick, P., Weakland, J., & Fisch, R. (1974). *Change: Principles of problem formation and problem resolution.* New York: Norton.

Weiner, B. (1985). An attributional theory of achievement motivation and emotion. *Psychological Review, 92,* 548–73.

———. (1990). Attribution in personality psychology. In L. Pervin (Ed.), *Handbook of personality* (pp. 465–83). New York: Guilford.

Weissman, M., Rounsaville, B., & Chevron, E. (1982). Training psychotherapists to participate in psychotherapy outcome studies. *American Journal of Psychiatry, 139:11,* 1442–46.

Weissmark, M., & Giacomo, D. (1988). *The Harvard Psychotherapy Coding Manual* (unpublished manuscript).

———. (1994). A therapeutic index: Measuring therapeutic actions in psychotherapy. *Journal of Consulting and Clinical Psychology, 62,* 315–23.

———. (1995). Measuring therapeutic interactions: Clinical and research applications. *Psychiatry: Interpersonal and Biological Processes, 58,* 173–88.

Wertheimer, M. (1978). Humanistic psychology and the humane but tough-minded psychologist. *American Psychologist, 33,* 739–45.

Wierzbicki, M. (1993). *Issues in clinical psychology.* Boston: Allyn & Bacon.

Wiley, M. G., & Alexander, C. N. (1987). From situated activity to self-attribution:

The impact of social structure schemata. In K. Yardley & T. Honess (Eds.), *Self and Identity: Psychosocial perspectives* (pp. 105–18). New York: Wiley.

Willett, J., Ayoub, C., & Robinson, D. (1991). Using growth modelling to examine systematic differences in growth: An example of change in the function of families at risk of maladaptive parenting, child abuse or neglect. *Journal of Consulting and Clinical Psychology, 59,* 38–47.

Wilson, G., Hannon, A., & Evans, W. (1968). Behavior therapy and the therapist-patient relationship. *Journal of Consulting and Clinical Psychology, 32,* 103–9.

Winograd, T., & Flores, F. (1986). *Understanding computers and cognition: A new foundation for design.* Reading, MA: Addison-Wesley.

Wolfe, B., & Goldfried, M. (1988). Research on psychotherapy integration: Recommendations and conclusions from an NIMH workshop. *Journal of Consulting and Clinical Psychology, 56,* 448–51.

Young, J. E., & Beck, A. T. (1982). Cognitive Therapy: Clinical applications. In A. J. Rush (Ed.), *Short-term psychotherapies for depression* (pp. 182–214).New York: Guilford.

Young, J. E., Beck, A. T., & Weinberger, A. (1993). Depression. In D. Barlow (Ed.), *Clinical handbook of psychological disorders* (pp. 240–77). New York: Guilford.

Zetzel, E. (1956). Current concepts of transference. *International Journal of Psychoanalysis, 37,* 369–76.

Index

interview techniques (*continued*)
   identifying assumptions, 126; inductive
   questioning, 124–25, 138; listening,
   130, 138; nondirective exploratory, 134,
   138; questioning validity of assumptions, 127, 138; responding to core
   theme, 131; understanding, 130–31;
   working through, 131–32, 138
intuition: concept of, 2, 14–15, 45–46; effective use of, 6, 139–41. *See also* analogical thinking
isomorphism, 55, 69

Jones, E., 35

Kagan, J., 95
Kaminer, W., 149
Kazdin, A., 17, 43
Kelly, G., 149–50, 153
Klerman, G., 133–34
knowing-in-practice: and clinical applications, 139–44; and clinical experience,
   45–47, 50–51; concept of, 40–42, 47–
   50, 56–60; method for defining, 5–6;
   and skillful ability, 44–45; versus theory,
   1–3, 7, 42–44, 122–23, 144–46. *See also*
   analogical thinking
knowing-in-theory: and clinical applications, 137–39; versus clinical competence, 42–44; and clinical experience,
   45–47, 50–51; concept of, 40–42, 47–
   50, 56–60; versus practice, 1–3, 7, 42–
   44, 122–23, 144–46; and skillful ability,
   44–45. *See also* logical thinking
knowledge: gained from practice, 2; types
   of, 40–42, 51–52, 58. *See also* analogical thinking; knowing-in-practice;
   knowing-in-theory; logical thinking

Lambert, M., 21
Landis, C., 15
Langer, E., 89
language: in analogical thinking, 53–54,
   59; in logical thinking, 52; of relational
   assessment, 68–69, 71–72
Lazarus, A. A., 26
LeDoux, J. E., 79
Leitner, L. M., 25

Likert scale, 33
listening, role of, 58, 130, 138
literature, and automatic assessments, 80–
   81, 96–97
literature reviews, evaluation of, 16–17
logical thinking: versus analogical thinking, 51–52, 56, 122; and clinical applications, 137–39; components of, 7; concept of, 52–53, 58–59; and descriptive
   attributes, 63. *See also* knowing-in-
   theory
loyalty, Othello's assessment of, 80–81
Luborsky, L.: on conflicts, 129; on core
   theme, 131; on patient's improvement,
   131–32; on personality system, 128; on
   therapeutic alliance, 49; therapies compared by, 16–17
Luborsky, Lise, 16–17
Luchins, A., 122

Maher, B., 6
maladaptive assumption, example of, 70–
   71. *See also* relational assessments
manuals: adherence to, 42–44, 48–49,
   57; problems with, 38; role of, 20–22,
   37, 43
Markman, H., 113
Marx, R., 118
matching–not matching variable: coding
   of, 110–14; description of, 104–5; and
   results, 107–8
mental attributes: concept of, 64–65,
   74–75; limits of, 65–68; measurement
   of, 65–66
meta-analytic techniques, 17–18, 28, 34
metaphor: in relational assessments,
   72–73; role of, 54–55, 59. *See also*
   analogy
methods: for rating therapeutic alliance,
   32–36; single-variable, 118. *See also* case
   study; Harvard Psychotherapy Coding
   Method (HPCM); treatment
Michotte, A. E., 66–67, 75
Minuchin, S., 109, 122
motivation theory, metaphor in, 54–55
multiple personality, research on, 11–12
Murray, H., 128
mutuality, in therapeutic alliance, 32